DISABILITY & HUMAN RIGHTS

An Overview

Dr. Vani Datt Sharma

INDIA • SINGAPORE • MALAYSIA

Contents

Introduction

The UN Charter underscores the importance of universal respect and adherence to human rights and essential liberties for all individuals, regardless of their physical or mental abilities. During the 1940s and 1950s, the UN concentrated on advocating for the rights of those with physical impairments through various social welfare strategies and programs within the disability sector. This period also saw the adoption of key international covenants on civil, political, economic, social, and cultural rights. As global awareness of disability rights grew, the General Assembly took further steps, including adopting declarations for the rights of individuals with mental disabilities and those with disabilities in general. The year 1981 was designated as the International Year for Disabled Persons, marking a significant milestone in disability advocacy.

Subsequently, numerous agreements and conventions have been organized to ensure the development of disability-focused policies and initiatives. These efforts aim to advance the social, economic, cultural, civil, and political rights of individuals with disabilities. The international community has been called upon to create action plans and programs that promote participation, inclusion, and enhanced quality of life for people with disabilities, while also combating their social exclusion.

Defining disability precisely has always been a formidable task, yet it remains crucial for proper identification and targeted implementation of international agreements, local legal benefits, and programs aimed at helping those with disabilities and the organizations supporting them. This definition is essential for creating accurate profiles, measuring disability, and advancing policies for their betterment. It's vital to view individuals with disabilities as subjects in their own right, not merely objects of charity or pity.

Disability must be addressed on two broad fronts: physical and mental. Physical disabilities encompass bodily impairments and disfigurements, while mental disabilities often stem from limited interaction and self-imposed restrictions due to societal attitudes encountered in daily life. This social disadvantage and activity limitation arise from discrimination, effectively excluding the person from mainstream activities. At the physical level, disability includes impairments that restrict major life activities. However, the mental aspect of disability, resulting from discrimination, inhibition, and subsequent exclusion from basic amenities like education, healthcare, and transportation, can be even more detrimental.

Disabilities can manifest in various forms - physical, cognitive, behavioral, or emotional. Despite the universal principle that all humans are born free and equal in dignity and rights, people with disabilities worldwide often face human rights violations, humiliation, and discrimination. Disability is a complex interplay between an individual's physical features and societal structures. It may be present from birth, result from an accident, or develop over time. The concept of disability encompasses past and present circumstances, as well as subjective perceptions. A disability can arise from a combination of impairments and environmental barriers, including attitudinal obstacles, inaccessible information, or other factors that hinder full societal participation. This comprehensive understanding of disability underscores the need for a multifaceted approach to addressing the challenges faced by individuals with disabilities.

The United Nations' Convention on the Rights of Persons with Disabilities (CRPD) acknowledges disability as a dynamic concept, arising from the interplay between individuals with impairments and societal barriers that impede their equal participation in society. Addressing both physical and mental aspects of disability has been the focus of international covenants and conventions, which various nations have incorporated into their legal frameworks. While legal systems can establish procedural foundations, broader societal awareness is crucial for integrating disabled individuals into the community. This study aims to highlight the human rights concerns of persons with disabilities, delving into the psyche of those with physical disabilities and exploring the mental dimensions of disability, which is considered a critical aspect of human rights research.

This research seeks to examine various facets of disabled persons' lives, including their daily living conditions and existing support systems at familial, governmental, and non-governmental levels. It aims to identify shortcomings that exacerbate the challenges faced by the disabled and propose methods to facilitate their lives despite natural or accidental disabilities. The study will conclude with recommendations for immediate governmental actions and societal awareness parameters. An effort has been made to identify and relate to differently-abled individuals through their abilities rather than their disabilities.

Objectives of Study

The primary objectives of this study include:

1. Developing educational programs and support services to ensure equal opportunities for people with disabilities within the community.
2. Advocating for adequate representation of disabled individuals in decision-making bodies affecting their lives.
3. Enhancing independent living skills for physically disabled persons.
4. Improving accessibility to public services and facilities for disabled people.
5. Creating and disseminating empowering information and training materials for use by disabled people at national and local levels.
6. Actively promoting the participation of persons with disabilities in all aspects of social, economic, political, and cultural life.
7. Analyzing their core problems and potential solutions.
8. Assessing their awareness levels and ways to improve them.
9. Identifying their abilities, capabilities, and limitations.
10. Examining how they cope with various situations and circumstances.

METHODOLOGY

As the present study aims to analyze and examine the problems and challenges of the disabled persons of Jalandhar, the methodology is descriptive, comparative and analytical. For this purpose the primary source include interview with the different categories of disabled persons, care-takers of NGOs, official document, legislative acts, international conventions and declarations. Published works of scholars in the form of books, articles, periodicals and newspapers, constitute the main secondary source of the data for this study.

RELEVANCE OF THE PRESENT STUDY

As pointed out in the earlier part, the hardship of the persons with disability is all pervasive and can be seen in each and every location barring some exceptions only, as such, the highlighting of the problem as well as the study of various social legal, emotional and financial aspect of the disability is quite crucial. The outcome of the present study can also be beneficial for the ultimate analysis of the different aspects of issues of disability and can pave way for identifying the possible solutions for the problem. The present study becomes of more relevance once we are able to identify the hindering blocks as well as the possible solutions and can create proper sensitization amongst the society at large qua the hardship being faced by the persons with disability and creating awareness amongst the state as well as non-state actors and N.G.Os. The approach of the book is applied, building on empirical evidence and using individual experiences of disability. In this introductory chapter, we seek to provide a common background for understanding the approach and scope of the following chapters.

CHAPTERISATION

The present study is divided into Six chapters.

- The first chapter of the study is of introductory nature. It outlines the area of the study. In this chapter relevance, scope of the study, objective, scope, methodology and chaptaerisation has been discussed.

- The second chapter deals with the Evolution & Development of human right. It illustrates the evolution of our fundamental human rights and its relevance in human society. It deals with the nature and scope of human rights today in all sectors.

- The Third chapter anlayzes the socio economic back ground of different categories of disabled persons. A background and survey of disabled persons has been undertaken. Socio economic factors influencing the attitude of an individuals has been examined which are the major concerns of disabled. Their major problems and their solutions are investigated in these conditions.

- The fourth chapter deals with Disabled & Legislations. It broadly describes the basic human rights of disabled individuals and to make aware of their rights.

- The fifth chapter illustrates various International Developments and Disability rights in which procedures were prescribed for upholding rights of disabled persons at all facets which is beneficiary for disabled persons.

- The Sixth chapter is about the findings and concrete conclusions of the study. Some vital suggestions are also part of this chapter.

Chapter 2

Evolution and Development of Human Rights

Human rights are fundamental freedoms inherent to all individuals by virtue of their humanity. These essential rights are often infringed upon for those lacking economic, physical, mental, social, or emotional resources. Since the dawn of human civilization, even primitive societies have acknowledged these intrinsic rights necessary for a dignified human existence. A right can be understood as a justified claim an individual possesses. Human rights are those bestowed upon people simply because they are human beings. Originally, the term "right" connoted purity, virtue, and innocence. Historically, rights have been categorized as natural or civil. Natural rights encompass the right to life, sustenance, shelter, and freedom of conscience. The modern usage of "human rights" as seen in the 1948 Universal Declaration of Human Rights hearkens back to the 18th-century concept of the "Rights of Man." While no specific definition exists in UN declarations or covenants, human rights are generally understood as those inherent to our nature and essential for our existence as human beings. The recognition of these natural rights has a long history, traceable to documents like the Magna Carta (1215), the Petition of Rights (1627), and the Bill of Rights (1688) in the UK. The French National Assembly's Declaration of Rights of Man (1789) influenced the US Constitution, and by the 19th century, these rights had become foundational principles in the constitutional law of modern civilized states.

JES Fewett, in "The Law of Nations" (1968), aptly described the declaration of human rights as the source from which other conventions and national constitutions protecting these rights have been derived.

This underscores the pivotal role of human rights in shaping legal frameworks across the globe. In the aftermath of World War II, the concept of human rights gained global recognition and importance. The League of Nations, an international body that preceded this era, had proven ineffective in preventing the Second World War, highlighting the need for a more healthy global organization. As countries began rebuilding their governments and economies post-war, there was a collective desire to prevent future global conflicts. This led to the establishment of the United Nations on October 24, 1945, founded by major powers including the United States, Soviet Union, China, France, and the United Kingdom. The UN's primary objectives were to maintain international peace, resolve disputes between nations, and address global economic and humanitarian issues. Within three years of its inception, the UN adopted the Universal Declaration of Human Rights in 1948, setting a benchmark for future treaties and agreements. This declaration outlined fundamental rights that every individual should possess. Subsequently, several important treaties were adopted under the UN framework, including:

1. International Covenant on Economic, Social and Cultural Rights (ICESCR) 1966
2. Convention on the Elimination of All Forms of Racial Discrimination (CERD) 1965
3. Convention Against Torture (CAT) 1984
4. Convention on the Rights of Child (CRC) 1989

These conventions inspired many countries to ratify and enact local laws protecting their citizens' human rights. In Europe, the Council of Europe was established in 1948 to promote unity, safeguard common ideals, and facilitate economic and social progress among member states. The European Convention on Human Rights, adopted in 1950, led to the creation of the European Court of Human Rights, aimed at protecting individuals from human rights violations in Europe. This convention has been notable for offering a high degree of individual protection. Since 1998, the court, based in Strasbourg, France, has employed full-time judges to address cases brought by member states or individuals against member states.

The United Nations Office of the High Commissioner for Human Rights defines human rights as inherent to all human beings, regardless of nationality, residence, sex, national or ethnic origin, color, religion, language, or any other status. This definition emphasizes the universal and non-discriminatory nature of human rights, asserting that all individuals are equally entitled to these fundamental rights. The concept of human rights has evolved over centuries, with universality as its core principle. This fundamental idea posits that all individuals are entitled to certain inalienable rights simply by virtue of being human. However, this universality remains a subject of debate and controversy in various contexts. The journey towards human rights has been a long struggle, aimed at achieving a life of dignity for all. Even today, in countries like India, marginalized groups such as women, children, Dalits, and bonded laborers continue to fight for their place in mainstream society. Despite these ongoing challenges, the world acknowledged human rights as an inherent aspect of humanity through the UN Charter of 1945.

The roots of human rights can be traced back to the Natural Rights theory, derived from Natural Law concepts proposed by ancient Greek Stoic philosophers and later developed by thinkers like Thomas Hobbes and John Locke. The American and French Revolutions further propelled the human rights movement. Internationally, the evolution of human rights is visible in documents like the Magna Carta, the English Bill of Rights, the French Declaration, and the American Bill of Rights.

The 20th century saw a manifestation of human rights philosophy with the adoption of the UN Charter (1945), the Universal Declaration of Human Rights (1948), and various International Covenants. These documents emphasized protection for specific groups and rights, including women's rights, abolition of slavery, racial equality, civil and political rights, economic, social and cultural rights, and children's rights. In India, the Constitution's drafters incorporated human rights for both citizens and non-citizens.

The Natural Rights Theory

The Natural Rights theory, a precursor to modern human rights, evolved from the concept of natural law, which was initially based on divine authority. This shift from natural law to natural rights represented a change in focus from society to the individual, providing a basis for limiting state power and enabling individuals to make claims against the government.

The modern conception of rights emerged during the Enlightenment, particularly in England, France, and the United States, as part of efforts to establish limited representative governments respecting individual freedoms. John Locke's "Second Treatise on Government" (1690) described a "state of nature" where individuals possessed natural rights to life, liberty, and property. This thinking influenced the founding fathers of the United States, as evident in the Declaration of Independence (1776), which stated:

> "We hold these truths to be self-evident, that all men are created equal, that they are endowed by their Creator with certain unalienable Rights, that among these are Life, Liberty and the pursuit of Happiness. —That to secure these rights, Governments are instituted among Men, deriving their just powers from the consent of the governed." This declaration marked a significant shift from the previous notion of divine right rule, establishing a new paradigm for understanding the relationship between individuals, governments, and rights.

The concept of human rights, while relatively recent in international law, has its roots in the doctrines of natural law and natural rights. These doctrines posited that individuals possess certain fundamental, inalienable rights that even sovereign states must respect.

Three key thinkers developed the Natural Rights theory: Thomas Hobbes (1588-1679), John Locke (1632-1704), and Jean-Jacques Rousseau (1712-1778). Thomas Hobbes, the pioneer of natural rights theory, argued in his seminal work "Leviathan" that the right to life, which humans enjoyed in the state of nature, was inviolable. He emphasized the inherent equality of all human beings, disregarding any other considerations. John Locke expanded on this idea in his "Two Treatises of Government." He contended that every individual possesses natural rights to life, personal liberty, and property. Locke maintained that these rights predated civil or political society, and thus, no governmental authority could legitimately deprive individuals of them. Jean-Jacques Rousseau, often considered the greatest proponent of the natural law school, famously stated in "The Social Contract" that "Man is born free, but everywhere he is in chains." Rousseau proclaimed that humans are endowed with the inalienable rights of liberty, equality, and fraternity. These concepts later formed the foundation of the French Declaration of the Rights of Man and of the Citizen.

This philosophical tradition of natural rights laid the groundwork for the modern understanding of human rights. It established the idea that certain fundamental rights are inherent to human beings, existing independently of and prior to any governmental or societal structures. This notion has profoundly influenced the development of human rights discourse and legislation, shaping our current understanding of the relationship between individuals and the state.

LANDMARKS IN DEVELOPMENT OF HUMAN RIGHTS

The important landmarks in the progress of human rights are as follows:

The evolution of human rights has been marked by several pivotal moments throughout history. These key developments have shaped our understanding and implementation of human rights today.

The Magna Carta of 1215

The Magna Carta of 1215 stands as a monumental constitutional document in human history. Its primary focus was to safeguard citizens against arbitrary royal actions. Comprising 63 clauses, it guaranteed fundamental civic and legal rights to citizens and shielded barons from unjust taxation. The English Church also gained freedom from royal interference. King John of England was compelled to grant this charter to the English barons on June 15, 1215, due to their refusal to pay heavy taxes without such protections.

The English Bill of Rights

The English Bill of Rights, enacted on December 16, 1689, by the British Parliament, marked another crucial step in human rights development. It firmly established parliamentary supremacy over the Crown, declaring that the monarch's authority was not absolute. This bill codified customary laws and elucidated citizens' rights and liberties, laying the foundations of legal supremacy and national sovereignty upon which the English constitution rests.

The American Declaration of Independence in 1776

The American Declaration of Independence in 1776 represented a significant milestone. On July 4, thirteen American colonies declared their independence from British rule, accusing the king of tyranny and affirming their autonomy. This declaration holds immense importance in human history as it justified the right to revolt against a government that failed to guarantee natural and inalienable rights.

The U.S. Bill of Rights

The U.S. Bill of Rights, ratified in 1791, addressed a notable omission in the original U.S. Constitution of 1787 – the lack of provisions for private rights and personal liberties. James Madison proposed twelve amendments, of which ten were ratified by state legislatures, becoming known as the Bill of Rights. The overarching theme of these amendments was to protect citizens against potential abuses of power by state officials.

These landmark documents collectively represent crucial steps in the progression of human rights, each building upon the principles of the previous and contributing to the framework of rights and liberties we recognize today. The evolution of human rights continued with several significant milestones in the late 18th and 20th centuries.

The French Declaration of the Rights of Man and of the Citizen

The French Declaration of the Rights of Man and of the Citizen, proclaimed on August 4, 1789, marked a new era following the fall of the Bastille and the abolition of feudalism. This 17-article declaration had far-reaching implications not only for France but for Europe and humanity at large. It effectively served as a death warrant for the old regime, introducing a new social and political order founded on noble principles. This declaration influenced many subsequent constitutions, with framers prioritizing human rights.

In the aftermath of World War I, discussions about human rights and fundamental freedoms gained prominence. The Institute of International Law adopted the Declaration of International Rights of Man in 1929, asserting that fundamental rights recognized in various domestic constitutions, particularly those of France and the USA, were intended for all people worldwide, without discrimination. The UN Charter of 1945, unanimously adopted by 51 states at the San Francisco Conference, marked the first official document to use the term 'human rights' and recognize respect for fundamental freedoms. This charter contains provisions for the promotion and protection of human rights. The Universal Declaration of Human Rights, adopted by the UN General Assembly on December 10, 1948, consists of 30 articles covering civil, political, economic, social, and cultural rights for all individuals. Although not legally binding, it serves as an ideal for all humanity.

To address the lack of enforceability in the Universal Declaration, the UN General Assembly adopted two International Covenants on Human Rights in December 1966: the International Covenant on Civil and Political Rights and the International Covenant on Economic, Social and Cultural Rights. These covenants, along with the Universal Declaration and Optional Protocols, comprise the International Bill of Human Rights, representing a modern Magna Carta of human rights and a milestone in human rights history. This progression of declarations and covenants illustrates the ongoing effort to codify, expand, and enforce human rights on a global scale, reflecting humanity's evolving understanding of fundamental freedoms and dignity.

HUMAN RIGHTS IN INDIA

India gained independence in 1947, just a year before the adoption of the Universal Declaration of Human Rights (UDHR). The architects of the Indian Constitution were cognizant that India's struggle for freedom was intertwined with the demand for basic human rights. Consequently, they incorporated certain rights as "fundamental rights" and delineated others as fundamental duties of citizens. The Supreme Court of India serves as the guardian of these rights as per the Constitution, considering fundamental duties when interpreting constitutional rights.

The Indian Constitution classifies rights into three primary categories: civil, political, and economic and social. Part III of the Constitution enshrines a set of individual rights termed "Fundamental Rights," emphasizing their essential nature. The Supreme Court of India recognizes these as "natural rights." Chief Justice Patanjali Shastri described them as "great and basic rights recognized and guaranteed as natural rights inherent in the status of a citizen of a free country," while Chief Justice Subha Rao referred to them as "the modern name for what has been traditionally known as natural rights." These Fundamental Rights are inviolable, meaning no law, ordinance, custom, usage, or administrative order can abridge or remove them. Any law violating these rights is void, binding both the legislature and executive. Even constitutional amendments cannot alter Fundamental Rights if they form part of the Constitution's basic structure. These rights are enumerated in Articles 12-35 of the Constitution, and their expansion must rely on judicial interpretation. The Constitution of India guarantees various civil, political, economic, social, and cultural human rights under the umbrella of "Fundamental Rights." Part III of the Constitution (Articles 12-35) provides a more comprehensive list of Fundamental Rights than any other existing written constitution. The 44th Amendment Act of 1979 classified these rights into six categories. Article 12 defines the "State" to include the Government and Parliament of India, state governments and legislatures, and all local or other authorities within Indian territory or under the control of the Indian Government. Article 13 imposes restrictions on violating fundamental rights, explicitly providing for judicial review of legislative enactments and executive actions to ensure their conformity with guaranteed fundamental rights. This constitutional framework reflects India's commitment to protecting and promoting human rights, rooted in its historical struggle for independence and aligned with global human rights developments.

The Indian Constitution enshrines the Right to Equality through Articles 14-18, encompassing several key principles:

Article 14 guarantees equality before law and equal protection of law. This means no individual should receive special state privileges, and all should receive equal treatment in equal circumstances. However, it also allows for treating unequal situations differently, as exemplified by the Supreme Court's recommendation to exclude the 'creamy layer' of Other Backward Classes (OBC) from reservation benefits.

Article 15 prohibits discrimination based on religion, race, caste, sex, or place of birth. It includes four main aspects:
1. General prohibition of discrimination
2. Equal access to public places
3. Protective measures for women and children
4. Reservation provisions for backward classes

Article 16 ensures equality of opportunity in public employment, comprising five clauses:
1. Equal opportunity in state employment
2. Prohibition of discrimination in state employment
3. Allowance for residential requirements in certain cases
4. Provision for protective laws for backward classes
5. Preference for certain persons in religious institutions

Article 17 uniquely abolishes untouchability and makes its practice or propagation punishable by law.

Article 18 abolishes titles, prohibiting the state from conferring any titles, except for military or academic distinctions.

These articles collectively aim to create a society based on equality and non-discrimination, while also allowing for protective measures for historically disadvantaged groups. They reflect India's commitment to balancing formal equality with substantive equality, recognizing the need for affirmative action in certain cases to address historical and social inequalities. The Right to Equality forms a cornerstone of Indian democracy, ensuring that all citizens are treated equally under the law while also providing for necessary safeguards and exceptions to promote social justice and inclusivity.

II. Right to Freedom (Articles 19 – 22)

a. Six fundamental freedoms - Article19

Article 19 (1), as amended by the Constitution (Forty Fourth) Amendment Act, 1979, guarantees to all citizens the following six freedoms:

- ➤ Freedom of speech and expression
- ➤ Freedom of peaceful assembly
- ➤ Freedom of forming associations or unions
- ➤ Freedom of movement throughout the territory of India
- ➤ Freedom of residence and settlement in any part of the territory of India, and
- ➤ Freedom of profession, occupation, trade or business.

b. Protection in respect of conviction for offences - Article20

This right guarantees protection in respect of conviction for offences, to those accused of crimes. There are three clauses to this article.

(i) Protection against ex – post, facto legislation – It means that a person cannot be punished under such a law, for his actions which took place before the passage of the law.

(ii) Protection against double punishment – it says that no person shall be prosecuted for the same offence more than once.

(iii) **Protection against self incrimination** – this clause states that no person accused of an offence shall be compelled to be a witness against himself.

18

c. **Protection of life and personal liberty - Article21**

Article 21 of the Indian Constitution recognizes the right to life and personal liberty. It provides that "no person shall be deprived of his life or personal liberty except according to procedure established by law."

d. **Protection against arrest and detention in certain cases. – (Article22)**

The provisions of Article 22 are complimentary to those of Article 21. Article 22 has two parts; the first part consisting of clauses (1) and (2), deals with persons, who are arrested under ordinary criminal law and the various rights, they are entitled to; and the second part consisting of the remaining clauses (3) to (7), is concerned with persons, who are detained under a law of preventive detention.

III. Right against Exploitation (Articles 23-24)

a. **Prohibition of traffic in human beings and forced labour – (Article23)**

The article prohibits traffic in human beings and *begar* and other similar forms of forced labour.

b. **Prohibition of employment of children – (Article24)** Article 24 of the constitution prohibits child labour. Children below fourteen years of age cannot be employed in any factory or mine or in any other hazardous employment.

IV. Right to Freedom of Religion (Articles 25 – 28)

a. **Freedom of Conscience and Religion - Article25** Article25 reflects the spirit of secularism and recognized freedom of religion to everyone in India.

b. **Freedom to manage religious affairs - Article26** It recognizes the right of every religious order to establish and maintain institutions for religious and charitable purposes and manage its own affairs in matters of religion.

c. **Freedom as to payment of taxes for promotion of any particular religion - Article27** The state shall not compel any person to pay any taxes for the promotion of maintenance of any particular religion or religious denomination.

d. **Freedom to attend religious instruction in education Institution - Article28**

This article prohibits imposition of religious beliefs by educational institutions on those who are attending them. Taken together the four Articles (25 to 28) establish the secular character of democracy.

V. Cultural and Educational Rights (Article 29-30)

a. **Cultural right of the individual as well if minorities - Article29**
This Article states that every section of the society has the right to conserve its distinct language, script or culture.

b. **Right of minorities to establish and administer Educational Institution - Article30**

The State cannot discriminate in granting aid to any educational institution on the ground that it is under the management of a religious or linguistic minority.

VI. Right to constitutional Remedies (Article 32)

Article 32 provides for the Constitutional Remedies, under which, one can move the Supreme Court for the enforcement of the Fundamental Rights and this provision itself is made one of the Fundamental rights. This is something unique. Dr. Babasaheb Ambedkar considered it as the very heart and soul of the constitution.

The other rights that are guaranteed in the Indian Constitution are as follows.

r.   **Right of property - Article31**

t.   **Power of Parliament to modify the right - Article33**

u.   **Restriction on right while martial law is in force- Article34**

v.   **Parliament empowered to make to enforce certain Fundamental Right - Article35**

By the 44th Amendment Act, 1978, the right to property was eliminated from the list of Fundamental Right. However though it is not a fundamental right, it is still a constitution at right. It is also a human right. This was recent ruling by the Supreme Court, while dismissing an appeal filed by the Karnataka Financial Corporation Challenged a State High Court order.

The Fundamental Rights in the Indian Constitution, outlined in Articles 14-35 of Part 3, can be categorized in several ways. The Constitution initially classified these rights into seven groups:

a)   Right to equality (Articles 14-18)

b)   Right to particular freedoms (Articles 19-22)

c)   Right against exploitation (Articles 23-24)

d)   Right to freedom of religion (Articles 25-28)

e)   Cultural and educational rights (Articles 29-30)

f)   Right to property (Article 31, now eliminated by the 44th Amendment)

g)   Right to constitutional remedies (Articles 32-35)

2.   Citizenship-based classification: Some rights are exclusively for citizens (Articles 15, 16, 19, and 30), while others apply to all persons, citizens or foreigners.

3.   Nature of rights: Some rights are prohibitions on state action (negatively expressed), such as Article 14's equality clause. Others confer benefits (positively worded), like the right to religious freedom in Article 25.

4.   Extent of limitation: Some rights limit executive power (e.g., Article 21), while others restrict legislative power. Rights in Articles 15, 17, 18, 20, and 24 impose absolute limitations, curbing even legislative authority.

5. Applicability: Most rights are guarantees against state action (e.g., Articles 19 and 21). However, some rights can be invoked against both the state and private individuals, such as the prohibition of untouchability (Article 17) and trafficking in human beings (Article 23).

This multifaceted classification of Fundamental Rights reflects the comprehensive approach of the Indian Constitution in safeguarding individual liberties and promoting social justice. It demonstrates the balance between universal rights and citizen-specific protections, as well as the interplay between state responsibilities and individual freedoms. The classification also highlights the Constitution's nuanced approach to addressing various aspects of civil liberties, social equality, and protection against exploitation.

Chapter 3

Socio Economic Background of Disabled Persons

As a part of this research, a study of the various factors concerning the socio economic aspects regarding the disability have been undertaken relating to dynamic interplays between disability and various aspects of culture and society. The point in issue relating to the socio economic background of the disabled is closely related to their place in the society. The social status as well as social participation of a disabled person depends substantially upon the economic standard of the disabled in a particular society and the means he has at his disposal to supplement and compliment his disability. While a resourceful person with disability with the supplementary measures at his disposal faces comparatively lesser level of hardship, embarrassment and harassment rather commands a respectful sympathy from the members of the society. On the contrary a not so fortunate person with disability and also having meager resources at his command has to face unbearable hardship as well as embarrassment, even meeting his both ends meet. The comparison becomes more unfortunate when it comes to assessing the public facilities and platforms by the persons with disabilities falling in these two different categories. A resourceful person with disability, who is able to have his own conveyance of whatever level it is, faces lesser level of hardship while a person with disability and having no conveyance at his disposal faces acute hardship in assessing public platforms transport and other facilities. In this whole process, both these categories come across absolutely different experiences and the resultant different attitudes are formed by the same class of persons with disabilities on the basis of their different experiences. Similarly the resourcefulness also describes the upbringing of the persons with disabilities at both levels. While education adds to the cart of resourceful person with disabilities and pushes him to a different level of opportunities in life, the lack of resources for education by the other disabled persons, rather adds to the miseries for coming life time. Similar is the state with regard to the matrimonial aspect and job opportunities of the same class of disabled who happen to be in different category of resources for one reason or the other.

Another crucial aspect, which has been studied by me is that disability in itself proves to be a hindrance in the overall development of the person except for some rare exception of education and resourcefulness. The persons with disabilities who had to manage the life on their own in routine end up making a living with difficulty and being at a loss of support even by the close relatives. However, there were some exceptions noticed where the persons with disabilities were member of joint families and the joint family took it up as a challenge to support the person with disability. Another significant factor has been the setting up of vocational training centers which influenced the economic and social status of the persons with disabilities by imparting them with sufficient training to earn a livelihood. Not only the imparting of the vocational training, these centers also arrange suitable employment of the persons with disabilities as per their ability, which has the effect of the raising socio economic aspect of the person with disabilities. Continuing upon this factor, the access to legal recourse as well as the proper availing of the opportunities by a person with disability also depend upon the economic resourcefulness, education of the concerned person. The persons with disability, Equal Opportunities Protection of Rights and Full Participation Act of 1995 had brought about a new dawn in the lives of disabled people in India. The act talked upon multiple needs of disabled people and provided 3% reservation in all the jobs of government and public undertakings. The legal implications of this act have been tremendous but it was a first step only. Even now the Ministry of Social Justice and Empowerment of the Govt. of India is of the process of holding National Consultative Meeting on proposed amendments to the said act.

Socio economic factors determine the variation in the participation of the disabled persons in the society as well in the nation. These are both the cause and effect in participatory difference between different facets of disabled people. Their behavior reflects a particular socio cultural milieu. It is weaved in by socio structure, their family background, professional consciousness, economic development, awareness level, their core problems and their solutions.

Socio Economic environment influences the personalities of the disabled person in the societal sphere to a great extent. The behavior, mannerism, values, their attitude, orientation, norms of the disabled persons are deeply shaped by the environment, so it is essential to have knowledge about the socio economic background of the disabled persons. The socio economic study plays vital role in forming the particular nature and moulding the behavior of a person living in particular environment. An analytical study of these factors will help to understand the environment and behavior, problems and their mannerism to cope up with those problems at various different stages. Majority of the disabled persons who are suffering from their disability have these problems from their birth and due to the negligence on the part of parents. The present study attempts to discuss pattern of disabled persons in the societal problems and their socio economic attributes. To compare the socio economic background of the disabled persons, important factors such as place of birth, age family background, education, cause of disability, problem being faced, challenges, awareness of the legislation etc needed to be critically analyzed.

During this study, the respondents were interviewed on a variety of themes, including their experiences, access to healthcare, public buildings, transportation, public spaces such as parks and sidewalks, and housing. Nearly all interviews were facilitated by local disabled persons organizations (DPOs), non governmental organizations (NGOs), or disability advocates. Since the focus of this report is on accessibility, the study has not included to interview people with psychosocial disabilities. People with psychosocial disabilities typically experience a range of challenges quite different from accessibility, including forced confinement and the absence of first hand account at the time of interview and can be part of a full fledged separate study.

This descriptive cross-sectional study was carried out on 10 different types of disabled persons Informed consent was obtained from the participants and the NGOs before the interview was conducted. The information sheet was explained to the participants and their queries were clarified. The study comprised different disabled persons of eighteen years and above. Since this population is difficult to access and were limited in numbers all consenting participants at these two settings that fulfilled the inclusion criteria were included in the study. In addition to questions on socio demographic characteristics, it had open-and close-ended questions to study their attitudes, difficulties faced during their movement, methods they used to overcome these difficulties, and their day to day hurdles.

Disability has many facets. First, it is important to understand that there are many different types and severities of impairment which lead to disabilities. Some types of impairment are: visual impairment, hearing impairment, movement impairment, cognitive/language impairment, seizure disorders. Within each of these major types, there are many variations and degrees of impairment. Each of these may present different barriers and need to be addressed with different strategies.

FAMILY BACKGROUND

The respondents had both single as well as joint family background. Some of them had responsible family background and which initially cooperated in all matters of all the respondents. Out of 10 few of them had cordial relations with their families. Their families were also cooperative with their children. Few of them were satisfied with their families. But there were others who showed dissatisfaction on their family responses. They blamed their families for so many reasons. Few of them did not know their families. They were there from immediately after their birth onwards. They were having their problems either due to birth or negligence of their families. All of them had left their families for so many reasons like – dissatisfaction, humiliation, frustration, disregard, over caring to be called as, "bechara", hesitation of attending families functions etc. They had negative as well as positive attitude towards their parents.

AIM OF LIFE

Out of 10 respondents few of them desired to be computer engineer, go in for their career in teaching, banking etc as they felt that they were just like any other common person. They don't think they have any such problem that they can't face the challenges of life. They had knowledge of all mechanisms to enter any type of jobs. Those who were visually impaired were more open, vocal and desired to achieve their goals and aspirations. They were aware of all the laws regarding their facilities and towards cause of their achievement.

SOURCE OF INCOME

All the respondents had no source of income from their family. Rather they don't have expectations from any source. They responded that they are fully supported by their NGOS. They had self-confidence, self reliant, determined to get jobs to earn their living. They were positive on this front. They had no burden of earning their livelihood.

ACHIEVEMENTS AND GOALS

Regarding their achievements and goals all the respondents had very positive responses to share. It was great to learn that despite having the disabilities, they were having positive attitude in their lives. One of the respondents who was visually impaired was very confident and energetic. He knew all the legislations concerning his disability given by the government to achieve their goals. There seemed no hurdle in their lives. He had vocational knowledge of computer training and on screen training software knowledge. He found no problem in functioning with latest technologies like JAWA Screen reader software and computer installation.

Another respondent who was visually impaired was doing Post graduation in Punjabi language and desired to go for teaching. He had cleared teacher's eligibility test and had done B.Ed. other respondent had done 5yrs music diploma (visharad double). Most of them had done computer course along with their basic qualification.

Many respondents said that they had faced discrimination in hiring and working conditions due to their disabilities, had missed out on professional development opportunities, and had been unable to find suitable employment. Unemployment affects people with disabilities disproportionately in comparison with the general population.

PROBLEM FACING

Many people with disabilities also mentioned multiple problems that prevent them from accessing transportation, entering train stations or bus stops, boarding transport, or communicating with transport operators. The lack of accessible transportation further segregates people with disabilities from the rest of society, making it difficult or impossible for them to see friends and family, work outside their homes, date, or enjoy public facilities and institutions, such as museums, theaters, and parks. Although governments have begun to provide accessible buses or taxis, many people interviewed said that they were too few in number, service was infrequent, and information was lacking about their schedules. Interviewees also described a dearth of accessible sidewalks and street crossings. Many people with physical disabilities whom interviewed said that they would like to work full time, go to school or be involved in their children's schools, socialize with friends, and enjoy public spaces

Lack of access to transport

People with sensory disabilities talked about a lack of access to make public transportation or services accessible. People with disabilities also said that they had trouble accessing healthcare facilities and services in part due to lack of access to adequate rehabilitation devices and services. In the case of people who are deaf or hard of hearing, they had difficulties communicating with healthcare professionals and getting emergency services. People with different disabilities noted that some healthcare workers refused to speak directly with them or accommodate basic accessibility needs. Those persons who were interviewed cited problems using rail, auto, and air transportation making it very difficult, or in some cases impossible, for them to get to work, socialize, go to school, or otherwise participate in society. One problem is the physical inaccessibility of transport stations and vehicles such as trains, metro cars, and buses. People with sensory disabilities reported insufficient or nonexistent visual and auditory clues on buses or in minibuses, in particular. Some interviewees also reported that transport operators seldom had any disabled friendly means of access and sometimes failed to accommodate people with disabilities, for example when bus drivers refused to lower wheelchair lifts to allow people to enter the vehicles.

Of the 10 cases I documented in which only a few respondents with disabilities or their legal guardians submitted written complaints to local authorities, half involved inaccessible public housing barriers to access to transportation, the role of education in access to employment

Limited Access to Subject Material

The vast majority of people with disabilities whom we interviewed either attended specialized schools for people with disabilities or studied at home, with teachers visiting them for several hours each week. Some people felt that they had received an adequate education in specialized schools but pointed out the limited range of subject material compared with mainstream schools.

For example, Lovepreet attended a specialized boarding school for children with visual impairments. He reported that at this school, students were given textbooks with large print, teachers were supportive, and he had friends. He report that certain subjects such as physics, which were available to his peers in mainstream schools, were not available in him specialized school but that he was, overall, satisfied with the community he formed and the knowledge he gained. He said, "The College did not prepare me for an education. I didn't know what to do afterwards."

Lack of opportunities to Education

People with disabilities reported a lack of opportunities to obtain vocational and higher education to prepare them for the jobs. Inclusive education "is the practice of educating students with disabilities in mainstream schools in their neighborhood."

Lack of Access to Healthcare and Rehabilitation

The people with disabilities who were interviewed reported a variety of obstacles accessing healthcare and rehabilitation facilities and services. These obstacles included difficulties accessing healthcare clinics and diagnostic equipment; a lack of rehabilitation facilities and appropriate healthcare specialists in or near peoples' communities; and a lack of knowledge of and access to rehabilitation devices and services. People who are deaf and hard of hearing also reported lack of access to emergency services and difficulties making appointments. Women with physical and sensory disabilities described healthcare workers' lack of respect for their right to found a family.

Lack of Access to Information Technology

Lack of information is a great problem for the majority of disabled people and is often under-rated as a cause of discrimination. Physical inaccessibility and lack of provision for people with visual, hearing and intellectual impairments drastically impedes disabled people's ability to learn about the world and their opportunities to take part in and to shape that world. The lack of representation of disabled people in decision-making processes and the lack of participation in all sections of society presents a barrier to development and social change.

Inadequate Communication

Communication is another area where there is not enough attention paid upon. People having communication barriers are the ones who face lot of hardships. Major communication barriers in the society include lack of Readers, Braille Material, Manuals, Magazines, Government Orders, Gazette, News Papers and Scribe Facility for people with Visual Impairment, lack of Sign Language & Sign Language Interpreters for People with Hearing Impairment, lack of Communication Aids and technical devices for people with severe disabilities and a lack of importance to research on Alternative & Augmentative Communication, which hinders a huge amount of human resource in contributing towards the development of the country. Apart from these, there is an immense need for disabled friendly curriculum and examination system, which involve a variety of options and adaptations. Apart from these, lack of self esteem, over protective parents, low access of skills, pensions and other government incentives, basic skills.

Making Buildings disabled friendly

Architectural barriers in buildings include lack of Ramps, Railings, Signage, Braille Print, Adequate Spacing, Slip Resistant Flooring, Accessible Toilets and Chairs, Switches, Shelves, Wash Basins, Taps & Telephone at an accessible height. This kind of infrastructure help disabled people to be at ease and do their routines with minimum or no support. Apart from becoming self-reliant, such an internal atmosphere boosts their self-confidence and avoids unnecessary delay.

EXPECTATIONS FROM GOVERNMENT

All the respondents had many expectations from the government and non governmental organizations. From the government side, respondents had viewed that -

- Reservations must increase and be implemented effectively.
- A hostel facility for disabled in all educational Institutes
- After 8th reader and writer must be provided
- Recorded book not speedy available
- Brail knowledge must be easily available
- Easy availability of reader
- Inconvenience from government must be curtailed
- Educational guidance and counseling
- Economic and social security must be provided
- Braille books must be available in Educational Institutions
- Awareness camps must be regular feature
- Disability certificate must be easily provided
- Travelling facilities to be improved
- Feasible transport facilities
- Voter card and Aadhar Id card must be made
- Enforcement of Participation rights and in Decision making bodies
- Tender care and affection
- More Employment opportunities
- More Blind schools
- Source of communications and Information Technology
- Actual survey method and criteria to be formed
- Attention towards Hygiene and sanitation
- Disability pension and other economic security to be implemented
- Old age pension
- Good infrastructure and Basic facilities must be provided
- Rehabilitation facilities
- More access to employment Benefits

Law and policies focus largely on requiring that businesses and organizations employ a certain number of people with disabilities without necessarily specifying what kinds of jobs are being created and the conditions under which people with disabilities will work. The vast majority of people with disabled either loses or has been denied jobs when employers learnt of their disabilities.

STRENGTH AND WEAKNESSES

All the respondents had responded well in this question. Out of 10, many a respondents had confidence, willpower and determination. They had equal knowledge of technical know how, computer knowledge, sports, study same, with difficulty only in mathematics but now it is possible to overcome this hurdle too.

They had some weaknesses too i.e. emotional, not practical policies, ineffective policies disappoint, disheartened, dissatisfied, arrogant, ignorance, ill treatment, lack family support, shyness and not confident, feel uncomfortable with unknown ones, shy of attending functions.

Chapter 4

The Disabled and the Legislations

Currently, individuals with disabilities constitute the largest minority globally, exceeding 650 million people, which amounts to 10 percent of the world's population. In India, more than 50 million people face various forms of disability. Despite constitutional guarantees ensuring their full spectrum of rights—civil, political, economic, cultural, and social—effective implementation has often fallen short. Persons with disabilities frequently encounter violations of their basic human rights and societal exclusion, particularly those with mental or psychological disabilities. Since the 20th century, awareness regarding disabilities has been increasing both nationally and internationally. Today, addressing disability issues transcends mere welfare concerns to encompass fundamental human rights. There is a growing demand for equal opportunities, full participation, and comprehensive rights protection from all perspectives.

India's Constitution is rooted in principles of social justice and human rights. The Preamble, Directive Principles of State Policy, and Fundamental Rights underscore the state's commitment to its citizens. These provisions advocate for a proactive role by the state in elevating the status of marginalized groups. For instance, Article 41 mandates that the state, within its economic capacity, ensure the right to work, education, and public assistance for those facing unemployment, old age, sickness, or disability. Article 46 specifically directs the state to promote the educational and economic interests of weaker sections of society, including Scheduled Castes, Scheduled Tribes, and protect them from social injustice and exploitation.

According to Census 2011, disabled individuals make up 2.21% of India's total population. Among them, 7.62% are children aged 0-6 years. India signed the United Nations Convention on the Rights of Persons with Disabilities and ratified it on October 1, 2007. The enactment of the Rights of Persons with Disabilities Act 2016 expanded recognized disabilities from 7 conditions to 21. The focus has shifted from viewing disabilities through a medical lens to a social or human rights perspective, emphasizing the societal responsibility towards inclusion.

Persons with disabilities have often faced challenging situations where their human rights were compromised without them realizing they had legal recourse. In the 1970s, the General Assembly acknowledged the growing concern for the human rights of persons with disabilities through declarations such as those on the Rights of Mentally Retarded Persons and Disabled Persons, and by designating 1981 as the International Year for Disabled Persons. In the 1980s, the human rights of persons with disabilities became integral to international policy, marking a shift from disability as a social welfare issue to one of rights.

The United Nations Decade of Disabled Persons (1983-1992) in the 1990s led to significant outcomes, including the adoption of the Standard Rules on the Equalization of Opportunities for Persons with Disabilities by the 48th session of the General Assembly in 1993. These rules continue to serve as an international human rights framework for designing disability-inclusive policies, evaluations, and economic cooperation efforts.

Throughout the early 1990s, major international conferences focused on development agendas that included action plans and programs stressing the participation, inclusion, and improved well-being of persons with disabilities. These efforts highlighted the necessity of a comprehensive human rights framework encompassing international norms and standards across social, economic, civil, cultural, and political fields. Such a framework not only benefits persons with disabilities but also advances the rights of all individuals within society.

The Constitution of India applies universally to all Indian citizens, regardless of their physical or mental condition. It guarantees justice, liberty of thought, expression, belief, faith, and worship, equality of status and opportunity, and promotes fraternity to all citizens, including those with disabilities. Education is a fundamental right for every citizen, and the Constitution mandates free and compulsory education for all children up to the age of 14 years. Indian health laws include provisions specifically addressing the needs of disabled individuals, as outlined in the Mental Health Act of 1987. Various marriage laws enacted by the government apply equally to disabled individuals across different communities.

The British Council's definition of disability focuses on social conditions that disadvantage individuals by not accommodating their needs for accessing opportunities on par with others. It identifies these conditions as human rights violations and instances of discrimination against disabled people. According to this definition, disability is described as the limitation of activities caused by a society that fails to consider individuals with impairments, thus excluding them from mainstream participation.

The United Nations Convention on the Rights of Persons with Disabilities (UN CRPD) defines persons with disabilities as those with long-term physical, mental, intellectual, or sensory impairments, which, when interacting with various barriers, may hinder their full and equal participation in society. The World Report on Disability 2011 summarizes disability as a complex, dynamic, multidimensional issue that is subject to varying interpretations.

The Rights of Persons with Disabilities Act, 2016, aligns its definition of disability with that of the UN CRPD. Additionally, it defines a "Person with Benchmark Disability" as someone with at least 40% of a specified disability. The Constitution of India applies uniformly to all legal citizens, regardless of their physical or mental health status. It guarantees fundamental rights to every citizen, including those who are disabled. These rights include justice, liberty of thought, expression, belief, faith, and worship, as well as equality of status and opportunity, and the promotion of fraternity.

Article 15(1) prohibits discrimination on grounds of religion, race, caste, sex, or place of birth, ensuring equal treatment for all citizens, including the disabled. Article 15(2) further ensures that no citizen, including those with disabilities, shall face any disability, liability, restriction, or condition in accessing shops, public restaurants, hotels, places of public entertainment, wells, tanks, bathing ghats, roads, or places of public resort funded by the government or dedicated to public use.

Special laws or provisions can benefit women, children, socially and educationally backward classes, Scheduled Castes, and Scheduled Tribes. Article 16 guarantees equality of opportunity in employment or appointment to any office under the State for all citizens, including the disabled, prohibiting any form of untouchability as per Article 17.

Under Article 21, every person, including the disabled, is guaranteed life and liberty. Article 23 prohibits human trafficking, including that of disabled persons, and bans beggary and other forms of forced labor, making such practices punishable by law. Article 24 prevents children, including those who are disabled, from working in factories, mines, or hazardous employments before the age of 14, even when employed by private contractors working for the government.

Article 25 grants every citizen, including the disabled, the right to freedom of religion, allowing them to practice and propagate their religion with proper regard to public order, morality, and health. No disabled person can be compelled to contribute taxes for the promotion or maintenance of any specific religion or religious group. No disabled individual shall be denied the right to use their language, script, or culture, to which they have a connection. Every disabled person has the right to approach the Supreme Court of India to uphold their fundamental rights, a privilege guaranteed under Article 32. Like non-disabled individuals, disabled persons cannot be deprived of their property without due process of law, even though the right to property itself is not considered a fundamental right. Any unlawful deprivation of property can be legally contested through appropriate legal action, seeking remedies such as damages. Similarly, upon reaching 18 years of age, every disabled person is entitled, like their non-disabled counterparts, to have their name included in the general electoral roll for their respective territorial constituency.

Constitutional Provisions

- Preamble: The Preamble aims to secure social justice, along with economic and political justice, for all citizens, ensuring equality of status and opportunity.
- Fundamental Rights: The core principle underlying all fundamental rights guaranteed by the Constitution is the dignity of the individual. These rights are equally applicable to persons with disabilities.
- Directive Principles: Article 41 urges the State to make effective provisions to secure the right to work, education, and public assistance in cases of unemployment, old age, sickness, and disability. Article 46 mandates the State to promote the educational and economic interests of weaker sections of society and protect them from social injustice and exploitation.

Relief of the Disabled falls under State jurisdiction (Entry 9 in List II) as per the Seventh Schedule. Welfare of the Disabled and mentally retarded is listed under item 26 in the Eleventh Schedule and item 09 in the Twelfth Schedule.

Education for the Disabled

The right to education is guaranteed to all citizens, including those with disabilities. Article 29(2) prohibits the denial of admission to any educational institution maintained or aided by the State on grounds of religion, race, caste, or language. Article 45 directs the State to provide free and compulsory education for all children, including disabled children, until they reach 14 years of age. No child can be refused admission to any state-funded educational institution based on religion, race, caste, or language.

Every child with a disability has the right to free education until the age of 18 in integrated or special schools. Adequate provisions such as transportation, removal of architectural barriers, and modifications in examination systems must be ensured for the benefit of children with disabilities. They are also entitled to free books, scholarships, uniforms, and other educational materials.

Special schools for children with disabilities should offer vocational training facilities, and non-formal education should be promoted. Teachers' training institutions should be established to develop necessary manpower. Parents have the right to seek redressal for grievances regarding the placement of their children with disabilities through appropriate forums.

Health Rights

Article 47 of the constitution mandates the Government to prioritize improving nutrition, raising living standards, and enhancing public health. It specifically advocates for the prohibition of intoxicating drinks and drugs that are harmful to health, except for medicinal purposes. The health laws of India include several provisions that cater to the needs of all citizens, including those with disabilities. Specific Acts, such as the Mental Health Act of 1987, outline provisions aimed at safeguarding the health of individuals, including those with disabilities.

Family Laws

Various marriage laws enacted by the Government apply uniformly to individuals from different communities, including the disabled. These laws stipulate conditions that may prevent a person, whether disabled or non-disabled, from entering into marriage. The rights and responsibilities of married parties, whether disabled or non-disabled, are governed by specific provisions outlined in various marriage Acts such as the Hindu Marriage Act of 1955, the Christian Marriage Act of 1872, and the Parsi Marriage and Divorce Act of 1935. Other Acts, including the Special Marriage Act of 1954 (for couples of different religions) and the Foreign Marriage Act of 1959 (for marriages outside India), also apply to the disabled. The Child Marriage Restraint Act of

1929, amended in 1978 to prevent child marriages, equally applies to the disabled. According to the Guardian and Wards Act of 1890 and the Hindu Minority and Guardianship Act of 1956, as well as under Muslim Law, a disabled person may not act as a guardian of a minor if the disability prevents them from fulfilling this responsibility.

Succession Laws for the Disabled

Under the Hindu Succession Act of 1956, applicable to Hindus, physical disability or deformity does not disqualify a person from inheriting ancestral property. Similarly, the Indian Succession Act of 1925, governing intestate and testamentary succession, does not exclude disabled individuals from inheriting ancestral property. This principle applies equally to Parsis and Muslims. Moreover, a disabled person has the right to draft a will, provided they understand the implications and consequences of their actions at the time of writing. For instance, individuals with intermittent mental capacity can create a will during lucid periods. Even blind individuals or those who are deaf and mute can legally draft wills if they comprehend the significance of their actions.

Labour Laws for Disabled

The Labour Laws for the Disabled do not explicitly outline the rights of individuals with disabilities, but there are provisions within related regulations and policies that address their relationship with employers.

Employment

Regarding employment, 3% of government job vacancies are reserved for people with disabilities, with 1% each allocated for those with blindness/low vision, hearing impairment, and locomotor disabilities/cerebral palsy. Schemes will be developed to facilitate the training, welfare, age relaxation, and creation of a barrier-free work environment for these individuals. Government-run and government-funded educational institutions must reserve at least 3% of their seats for students with disabilities. Employees cannot be terminated or demoted if they acquire a disability during their service, though they may be transferred to a different position with the same pay and conditions. Promotions cannot be denied due to an employee's impairment.

Prevention and early detection of disabilities

To prevent and detect disabilities early, surveys, investigations, and research will be conducted to identify the causes. Primary healthcare workers will be trained to assist in this effort, and all children will be screened annually to identify 'at-risk' cases. Awareness campaigns will be launched to disseminate information, and measures will be taken to ensure proper prenatal, perinatal, and postnatal care for mothers and children. Regarding judicial procedures for the disabled, under the Designs Act of 1911, which governs the protection of designs, the court can appoint a person to act on behalf of a disabled individual who is incapable of making statements or performing actions required by the Act. This disability could be due to lunacy or other incapacitating conditions. In terms of income tax concessions and relief for the handicapped, Section 80DD of the tax code provides for deductions related to the medical treatment, including nursing, training, and rehabilitation of disabled dependents for individual taxpayers and Hindu Undivided Families residing in India.

The Persons with Disabilities (Equal Opportunities, Protection of Rights and Full Participation) Act of 1995 came into force on February 7, 1996, marking a significant step towards ensuring equal opportunities and full participation of people with disabilities in nation-building. The Act addresses both preventive and promotional aspects of rehabilitation, such as education, employment, vocational training, reservation, research, manpower development, the creation of barrier-free environments, rehabilitation of persons with disabilities, unemployment allowance for the disabled, special insurance schemes for disabled employees, and the establishment of homes for those with severe disabilities.

Legal Provisions

- **The Mental Health Act, 2017**: It replaced the Mental Health Act, 1987. It has been passed with the objective to provide for mental healthcare and related services for persons with mental illness and to protect, promote and fulfill their rights.

- **The Rights of Persons with Disabilities (RPwD) Act, 2016**: It came into force in April 2017. It replaced the Persons with Disabilities (Equal Opportunities, Protection of Rights and Full Participation) Act, 1995. It fulfils the obligations to the United National Convention on the Rights of Persons with Disabilities (UNCRPD). The Act has several provisions for benefit of persons with disabilities like it has **increased the magnitude of reservation** for Persons with Disabilities from 3% to 4% in government jobs and from 3% to 5% in higher education institutes. It stresses to **ensure accessibility** in public buildings in a prescribed time frame.

- **The Rehabilitation Council of India Act, 1992**: It provided statutory status to the Rehabilitation Council of India (RCI, established in 1986). The mandate given to RCI is to **regulate and monitor services given to persons with disability**, to standardise syllabi and to maintain a Central Rehabilitation Register of all qualified professionals and personnel working in the field of Rehabilitation and Special Education.

- **The National Trust for the Welfare of Persons with Autism, Cerebral Palsy, Mental Retardation and Multiple Disabilities Act, 1999**: It has been enacted with the objective to provide for the constitution of a body at the National level for the Welfare of Persons with Autism, Cerebral Palsy, Mental Retardation and Multiple Disabilities. The trust aims to provide total care to persons with mental retardation and cerebral palsy and also manage the properties bequeathed to the Trust. The Trust strives to enable persons with disability to live independently by: **(a)** Promoting measures for their protection in case of death of their parents; **(b)** Evolving procedures for appointment of their guardians and trustees; **(c)** Facilitating equal opportunities in society.

Welfare Programs

The Accessible India Campaign, launched in December 2015, aims to create a barrier-free and conducive environment for persons with disabilities across the country. It is based on the social model of disability, which recognizes that disability is caused by societal organization rather than individual limitations. The campaign targets three key areas: built-up environments, transportation ecosystems, and information and communication technology (ICT) ecosystems.

The Deendayal Disabled Rehabilitation Scheme (DDRS) aims to create an enabling environment to ensure equal opportunities, equity, social justice, and empowerment for persons with disabilities. Under this scheme, financial assistance is provided to non-governmental organizations (NGOs) to run projects for the rehabilitation of persons with disabilities, including special schools, pre-schools, early intervention programs, halfway homes, and community-based rehabilitation.

The Assistance to Disabled Persons for Purchase/Fitting of Aids and Appliances (ADIP) scheme aims to help needy disabled individuals procure durable and scientifically manufactured assistive devices. This promotes their physical, social, and psychological rehabilitation, reducing the effects of disabilities and enhancing their economic potential. The scheme is implemented by NGOs, national institutes under the Ministry of Social Justice and Empowerment, and ALIMCO, a public sector undertaking that manufactures artificial limbs.

The Indian Sign Language Research and Training Centre promotes the use of sign language and develops human resources in this field.

The National Institute of Mental Health Rehabilitation (NIMHR) aims to build capacity in the field of mental health rehabilitation and develop community-based rehabilitation protocols to mainstream persons with mental illness who have been successfully treated.

Social Security

In terms of social security, the government provides financial assistance to NGOs for the rehabilitation of persons with disabilities, insurance coverage for government employees with disabilities, and unemployment allowance to registered persons with disabilities who have been unable to find gainful employment for over a year.

Grievance Redressal

If a person with a disability experiences a violation of their rights as prescribed in the relevant act, they can submit an application to the Chief Commissioner for Persons with Disabilities at the central level or the Commissioner for Persons with Disabilities at the state level.

Mental Health Act, 1987

The Mental Health Act, 1987 grants several rights to mentally ill persons in India:

They have the right to be admitted, treated, and cared for in psychiatric hospitals, nursing homes, or convalescent homes established or maintained by the government or any other entity. This right extends to mentally ill prisoners and minors as well.

Minors under 16 years, persons addicted to alcohol or drugs leading to behavioral changes, and those convicted of an offense have the right to admission, treatment, and care in separate psychiatric facilities established or maintained by the government.

Mentally ill persons have the right to receive regulated, directed, and coordinated mental health services from the government. The central and state authorities set up under the act are responsible for this regulation and for issuing licenses to establish and maintain psychiatric hospitals and nursing homes.

Treatment can be obtained either as an inpatient or an outpatient at the government-run facilities mentioned above. Mentally ill persons can seek voluntary admission, and minors can be admitted through their guardians. Relatives can also apply on behalf of the mentally ill person, and the local magistrate can issue reception orders.

The police have an obligation to take a wandering or neglected mentally ill person into protective custody, inform their relatives, and produce them before the local magistrate for issuing a reception order.

Mentally ill persons have the right to be discharged when cured and to leave the mental health facility in accordance with the provisions of the act.

If a mentally ill person owns property that they cannot manage themselves, the district court can protect and secure the management of such property by entrusting it to a 'Court of Wards', appointing guardians, or appointing property managers.

Costs of Maintenance for Mentally Ill Persons

The costs of maintaining mentally ill persons admitted as inpatients in government psychiatric hospitals or nursing homes shall be borne by the state government, unless the costs have been agreed to be covered by the relative or other person on behalf of the mentally ill person, or if provision for such maintenance has been made by order of the district court. These costs can also be paid from the estate of the mentally ill person.

Protections for Mentally Ill Persons

Mentally ill persons undergoing treatment shall not be subjected to any physical or mental indignity or cruelty. They cannot be used for research purposes without their valid consent, though they can receive necessary diagnosis and treatment. Mentally ill persons entitled to any pay, pension, gratuity, or other government allowance (such as government servants who become mentally ill during their tenure) cannot be denied these payments. The person in charge of the mentally ill person or their dependents will receive such payments after the magistrate has certified the same.

A mentally ill person shall be entitled to the services of a legal practitioner, as ordered by the magistrate or district court, if they have no means to engage a lawyer or their circumstances warrant it for proceedings under the act.

Measures to Prevent Disability

Various measures shall be taken to prevent disabilities, including:

- Training staff at Primary Health Centers to assist in this work
- Screening all children once a year to identify 'at-risk' cases
- Launching awareness campaigns to disseminate information
- Providing pre-natal, peri-natal, and post-natal care for mothers and children
- Rights of Children with Disabilities
- Every child with a disability shall have the right to free education up to age 18 in integrated or special schools. Appropriate transportation, removal of architectural barriers, and modifications to the examination system shall be ensured for their benefit.
- Children with disabilities shall have the right to free books, scholarships, uniforms, and other learning materials. Special schools for children with disabilities shall be equipped with vocational training facilities, and non-formal education shall be promoted for them.
- Teacher training institutions shall be established to develop the required personnel. Parents may approach appropriate forums to address grievances regarding the placement of their children with disabilities.

Affirmative Action

Aids and appliances shall be made available to people with disabilities. Land shall be allotted at concessional rates for their houses, businesses, recreational centers, schools, research institutions, and factories run by entrepreneurs with disabilities.

Non-Discrimination

Public buildings, rail compartments, buses, ships, and aircraft will be designed to provide easy access for people with disabilities. Toilets in public places and waiting rooms shall be wheelchair-accessible, and Braille and audio indicators will be provided in elevators.

Research and Manpower Development

Research shall be sponsored and promoted in areas like prevention of disability, rehabilitation (including community-based), and development of assistive devices. Financial assistance will be provided to universities, higher learning institutions, professional bodies, and NGO research units for such research and manpower development.

The Rehabilitation Council of India Act, 1992

This act provides the following guarantees:

- Right to be served by trained and qualified rehabilitation professionals registered with the Council
- Maintenance of minimum standards of education for recognition of rehabilitation qualifications
- Maintenance of standards of professional conduct and ethics by rehabilitation professionals
- Regulation of the rehabilitation profession by a statutory council under the central government

The National Trust for Welfare of Persons with Autism, Cerebral Palsy, Mental Retardation and Multiple Disability Act, 1999

The central government is obligated to set up the National Trust in New Delhi to ensure the fulfillment of the objects enshrined in the act. The Board of Trustees must make arrangements for an adequate standard of living of beneficiaries and provide financial assistance to registered organizations for approved programs benefiting the disabled. Disabled persons have the right to be placed under guardianship appointed by the 'Local Level Committees' as per the provisions of the Act. The appointed guardians are responsible for the disabled person and their property, and must be accountable for the same. A disabled person has the right to have their guardian removed under certain conditions, such as abuse, neglect, or misappropriation of property. If the Board of Trustees of the National Trust is unable to perform or persistently defaults on their duties, a registered organization for the disabled can complain to the central government to have the Board superseded and/or reconstituted.

The National Trust is bound by the Act's provisions regarding its accountability, monitoring of finances, accounts, and audits.

The main idea is that the Act provides mechanisms for appointing guardians for disabled persons, holding guardians accountable, and allowing for grievance redressal if the National Trust fails in its duties. The writing style preserves the authoritative and informative tone of the original text.

UN Declaration on the Rights of Mentally Retarded Persons

The UN Declaration on the Rights of Mentally Retarded Persons calls for national and international actions to ensure its use as a common basis and frame of reference for protecting the rights of the mentally retarded. The mentally retarded person has, to the maximum feasible degree, the same rights as other human beings. This includes the right to proper medical care, physical therapy, education, training, rehabilitation, and guidance to enable them to develop their abilities and reach maximum potential. They have a right to economic security, a decent standard of living, and the ability to perform productive work or participate in meaningful occupations. Whenever possible, they should live with their own family or foster family and participate in community life, with support provided to the family. If institutional care is necessary, it should resemble a normal lifestyle as closely as possible. The mentally retarded person has a right to a qualified guardian when required to protect their personal well-being and interests. They have a right to protection from exploitation, abuse and degrading treatment, as well as the right to due process if prosecuted for an offense.

When rights must be restricted due to the severity of the handicap, proper legal safeguards against abuse must be in place, based on evaluations by qualified experts and subject to periodic review and appeal. Globally, it is estimated that 10% of the population suffers from disabilities, with 2.13% of the Indian population having disabilities according to the 2001 census, though estimates range up to 5-6%. The majority live in rural areas, and women make up over 42% of the disabled population.

International Commitments

India has signed on to several international frameworks and declarations related to the rights of persons with disabilities, including the Declaration on the Full Participation and Equality of People with Disabilities in the Asia Pacific Region, the Biwako Millennium Framework for Action, and the UN Convention on the Protection and Promotion of the Rights and Dignity of Persons with Disabilities. The Persons with Disabilities (Equal Opportunities, Protection of Rights and Full Participation) Act of 1995 was enacted to implement the Proclamation on Full Participation and Equality in the Asia-Pacific region. The National Policy for Persons with Disabilities of 2006 also reflects these international commitments, which aim to realize the economic, social and cultural rights of persons with disabilities.

India ratified the UN Disability Rights Convention in 2007, and is now in the process of designating a framework to promote its implementation. This will be integrated into the 11th Five Year Plan, providing a policy framework for the next five years and enabling cross-sectoral convergence in realizing disability rights. According to the 2011 Census, the differently abled population in India is 26.8 million, or 2.21% of the total population. This represents a marginal increase from 21.9 million in 2001. The disabled population is predominantly male (14.9 million) compared to female (11.9 million), and is concentrated more in rural areas (18.0 million) than urban (8.1 million). The Department of Empowerment of Persons with Disabilities in the Ministry of Social Justice & Empowerment is responsible for facilitating the empowerment of this population, which encompasses various types of disabilities.

The Constitution of India provides a strong foundation for developing legal instruments to protect the rights of persons with disabilities. The Preamble seeks to secure justice, liberty, equality, and dignity for all citizens. The Fundamental Rights enumerated in Part III of the Constitution, including the right to equality, freedom, and constitutional remedies, are also applicable to persons with disabilities, even though they are not explicitly mentioned.

Furthermore, the Constitution directs the State to make provisions for securing the right to work, education, and public assistance in cases of disability and other forms of deprivation. Article 46 also obligates the State to promote the educational and economic interests of weaker sections, including persons with disabilities, and protect them from social injustice and exploitation. While disability is a state subject under the legislative distribution of powers, the Constitution empowers the Parliament to legislate on any subject to fulfill India's international obligations. This includes the provisions in the Eleventh and Twelfth Schedules, which recognize the need to safeguard the interests of the disabled and mentally challenged.

Overall, the Indian Constitution provides a robust framework for the protection and empowerment of persons with disabilities, both through the Fundamental Rights and the directive principles of state policy. This serves as the foundation for the legal and policy measures enacted by the government to uphold the rights and inclusion of this population

Types of Disabilities as Per the PwD Act 2016 (Classification and Definition)

1. Blindness: Defined as complete darkness in vision, where individuals struggle to differentiate between darkness and bright light in either eye.
2. Low Vision: Refers to conditions where individuals may have: • Visual acuity not exceeding 6/18, or less than 20/60 up to 3/60 or up to 10/200 (Snellen) in the better eye with optimal corrections. • Field of vision limited to an angle of less than 40 degrees up to 10 degrees.
3. Leprosy Cured Individuals: Leprosy, a chronic infectious ailment, primarily affects the skin, peripheral nerves, mucosal surfaces of the upper respiratory tract, and the eyes.
4. Hearing Impairment (Deaf and Hard of Hearing): Characterized by partial or total inability to hear, classified into deaf and hard of hearing categories based on the degree of hearing loss in speech

frequencies. • "Deaf" denotes individuals with a 70 dB loss. • "Hard of Hearing" signifies a 60 dB to 70 dB loss in speech frequencies.

5. Locomotor Disability: A condition that impedes moving from one place to another, commonly associated with bone, joint, and muscle disorders affecting mobility and everyday activities.

6. Dwarfism: A growth anomaly resulting in individuals having a height below 4 feet 10 inches, characterized as dwarfism.

7. Intellectual Disability: Individuals experiencing limitations in essential life and community skills, encompassing communication, self-care, social interactions, safety, and self-direction.

8. Mental Disorders: A collective term for illnesses impacting mental and brain functions, such as bipolar disorder, depression, schizophrenia, anxiety, and personality disorders, affecting cognitive and emotional processes.

9. Autism Spectrum Disorder: An umbrella term encompassing various autism conditions, influencing information processing and storage in the brain, predominantly affecting communication, social interactions, and daily activities.

10. Cerebral Palsy: A disabling condition caused by impaired muscle coordination due to brain damage at or before birth, non-progressive in nature.

11. Muscular Dystrophy: A group of genetic neuromuscular disorders causing muscle weakness and loss of muscle mass, progressive with time.

12. Chronic Neurological Conditions: Including Alzheimer's disease, Parkinson's disease, dystonia, ALS (Lou Gehrig's disease), Huntington's disease, neuromuscular diseases, multiple sclerosis, and epilepsy, necessitating varied healthcare services for symptom management.

13. Specific Learning Disabilities (Dyslexia): Impairments hindering learning, listening, thinking, speaking, writing, spelling, and mathematical abilities, with examples like Dyspraxia, Dysgraphia, Dyscalculia, and ADHD.

14. Multiple Sclerosis: A CNS condition impeding information flow within the brain and body, with symptoms like fatigue, weakness, pain, stiffness, cognitive impairments, and more.
15. Speech and Language Impairment: Resulting from conditions affecting speech and language components due to organic or neurological causes.
16. Thalassemia: A genetically inherited blood disorder leading to abnormal hemoglobin production, causing anemia symptoms.
17. Hemophilia: A blood disorder marked by a deficiency in clotting proteins, resulting in prolonged bleeding.
18. Sickle Cell Disease: Causes RBCs to become sickle-shaped, leading to various health complications.
19. Multiple Disabilities, including Deaf-Blindness: The occurrence of multiple physical or mental disabilities simultaneously.
20. Survivors of Acid Attacks: Individuals, mostly women, victimized by acid throwing crimes, often leading to severe facial and bodily disfigurements.
21. Parkinson's Disease: A CNS disorder impacting movement, characterized by tremors and stiffness, with a progressive nature.

Landmark Judgements pertaining to Rights of Persons with Disabilities

Supreme Court Judgments

Deaf Employees Welfare Association v Union of India 2013 A petition was submitted requesting a Writ of Mandamus to instruct the Central and state governments to provide equal transport allowance to government employees with hearing impairments, similar to what was being given to blind and other disabled government employees. The transport allowance provided to employees with hearing impairments was significantly lower compared to those given to other disabled employees.

In response, the Supreme Court granted the petition and mandated the Respondents to extend transport allowance to individuals with speech and hearing impairments at par with blind and orthopedically disabled government employees. The court emphasized that discrimination between individuals with different disabilities, such as 'blindness' and 'hearing impairment,' was not justified under the Disabilities Act. It stressed the importance of ensuring equal treatment and protection under the law for all individuals with disabilities participating in government activities. The court further asserted that the dignity of individuals with hearing impairments must be safeguarded by the state, rejecting the notion that hearing or speech impaired individuals should receive lesser benefits than blind individuals. Any actions taken by the state to uphold this principle were in alignment with the constitutional principles outlined in Article 14. The ruling established that individuals who are deaf and mute should receive transportation allowances on par with blind and orthopedically disabled government employees.

Union of India v National Federation of the Blind (2013) 2 SCC 772 This case involved an appeal against a decision by the Delhi High Court regarding a public interest petition seeking the enforcement of Section 33 of the Act, alleging that the appellants had not provided reservations for blind and visually impaired individuals, resulting in their exclusion from government job recruitment processes as mandated by the Act.

The court examined the interpretation of the 3% reservation requirement – whether it applied to cadre strength or the number of vacancies. It clarified that the 3% reservation pertained to a portion of the total vacancies within the cadre strength. Additionally, the court highlighted that while Section 33 stipulates a minimum representation of 3% in government establishments, the legislature aimed to ensure a 5% representation across the entire workforce, encompassing both public and private sectors.

Government of India v Ravi Prakash Gupta (2010) 7 SCC 626

In this case, the respondent was a visually challenged person who appeared for the civil services examination conducted by the Union

Public Service Commission and was declared successful. However, he was not given an appointment even though he was at Sl. No. 5 in the merit list of visually impaired candidates. The respondent approached the Central Administrative Tribunal which refused his application and thereafter the respondent approached the high court. The high court directed the government to accommodate the Respondent in the merit list, against which the state filed an appeal in the Supreme Court. The state contended that since the post for which the respondent was applying was not identified for persons with disabilities and therefore not reserved for them, the government could not make reservations in the same. The Supreme Court refused the state government's contention that identification of jobs was a pre-requisite for reservation and appointment under section 33 of the Persons with Disabilities Act, 1995. The court held, "It is only logical that, as provided in section 32 of the aforesaid Act, posts have to be identified for reservation for the purposes of Section 33, but such identification was meant to be simultaneously undertaken with the coming into operation of the Act, to give effect to the provisions of Section 33. The legislature never intended the provisions of section 32 of the Act to be used as a tool to deny the benefits of Section 33 to these categories of disabled persons indicated therein. Such a submission strikes at the foundation of the provisions relating to the duty cast upon the appropriate government to make appointments in every establishment."

Syed Bashir-ud-Din Qadri v. Nazir Ahmed Shah (2010) 3 SCC 603

The Supreme Court observed that, "This case involves a beneficial piece of social legislation to enable persons with certain forms of disability to live a life of purpose and human dignity. This is a case which has to be handled with sensitivity and not with bureaucratic apathy, as appears to have been done as far as the appellant is concerned… It is only to be expected that the movement of a person suffering from cerebral palsy would be jerky on account of locomotor disability and that his speech would be somewhat impaired but despite the same, the legislature thought it fit to provide for reservation of 1 per cent of the vacancies for such persons. So long as the same did not impede the person from discharging his duties efficiently and without causing prejudice to the children being taught, there could, therefore, be no reason for a rigid approach to be taken not to continue with the appellant's services as Rehbar-e-Taleem, particularly, when his students had themselves stated that they had got used to his manner of talking and did not have any difficulty in understanding the subject being taught by him… Coupled with the above is the fact that the results achieved by him in the different classes were extremely good; his appearance and demeanour in school had been highly appreciated by the committee which had been constituted pursuant to the orders of the high court to assess the appellant's ability in conducting his classes."

The court directed that in order to overcome the impediment of writing on the black board, an electronic external aid could be provided to the appellant, which could eliminate the need for drawing a diagram and the same could be substituted by a picture on a screen, which could be projected with minimum effort. With these directions for providing reasonable accommodation, the Supreme Court held that the disengagement of the appellant goes against the grain of the PWD Act and hence the order was set aside by the court.

Suchita Srivastava v. Chandigarh Administration 2009 (9) SCC 1

This case was with regard to the reproductive rights of a woman with mental retardation residing at a government run welfare institution in Chandigarh who became pregnant due to a rape by an in-house staff and who wanted to keep the baby and carry on the pregnancy to full term. The Chandigarh Administration filed a petition in the high court seeking permission to terminate her pregnancy under the Medical Termination of Pregnancy Act, 1971 ("MTP Act") on the ground that she was not capable of carrying on with the pregnancy and would not be able to look after a child.

Although the expert body found that the woman had expressed her wish to bear her child, the high court directed the termination of the pregnancy. The woman, through an amicus, appealed to the

Supreme Court and one of the main issues before the Supreme Court was regarding the legal capacity of a woman with mental retardation to decide on her pregnancy. The Supreme Court noted the provisions of the MTP Act, which provided that where pregnancy is a result of rape and termination of the same is contemplated, the consent of the pregnant woman is mandatory. The court also noted the exception to this provision which provided that in case of a pregnant woman who is "mentally ill", pregnancy can be terminated with the approval of the woman's guardian. Following this, the court proceeded to make a distinction between 'mental illness' and 'mental retardation'. Upholding the legal capacity of the appellant, the court held: "While a guardian can make decisions on behalf a 'mentally ill person' as per Section 3(4)(a) of the MTP Act, the same cannot be done on behalf of a person who is in a condition of 'mental retardation'.

The only reasonable conclusion that can be arrived at in this regard is that the State must respect the personal autonomy of a mentally retarded woman with regard to decisions about terminating a pregnancy. It can also be reasoned that while the explicit consent of the woman in question is not a necessary condition for continuing the pregnancy, the MTP Act clearly lays down that obtaining the consent of the pregnant woman is indeed an essential condition for proceeding with the termination of a pregnancy.

Thus, the Supreme Court clearly held that the MTP Act required the consent of a mentally retarded woman for termination of pregnancy. Following this, the Court concluded that the Appellant was mentally retarded, had not consented to the termination of her pregnancy and in fact, had expressed her willingness to bear the child. Therefore, it could not permit the termination of her pregnancy. In arriving at this conclusion, the Court not only recognised the reproductive rights of a woman under the MTP Act, but also recognised international norms and principles on mentally retarded persons and persons with disabilities under the CRPD. Therefore, the Supreme Court laid out the specific right to legal capacity which was not subject to an understanding of one's situation and capacities. This case clearly follows the spirit of protection of legal capacity under Article 12 of the CRPD, 2006.

High Court Judgments

Ranjit Kumar Rajak v. State Bank of India (2009) 5 Bom CR 227

In an extremely significant ruling, a Division Bench of the Bombay High Court articulated and recognised for the first time the concept of "reasonable accommodation at the workplace" in India. The court relied on the CRPD 2006 to decide the duty of the employer in providing reasonable accommodation and the limits on such a duty. The court recognised that India had signed and ratified the CRPD, and that Article 27 of the Convention recognises the right of persons with disability to be "accepted in the labour market and work environment that is open, inclusive and accessible to persons with disabilities."

The court also discussed the definition of "reasonable accommodation" under Article 2 as "a necessary and appropriate modification and adjustments not imposing a disproportionate or undue burden, where needed in a particular case, to ensure to persons with disabilities the enjoyment or exercise on an equal basis with others of all human rights and fundamental freedoms."

In interpreting "reasonable accommodation" and "undue burden" the court relied on the CRPD and recognised the importance of India's international obligations with respect to rights of disabled persons by stating that: "The law is now well settled that though the United Nations Convention may not have been enacted into the Municipal Law, as long as the convention is not in conflict with the Municipal Law and can be read into Article 2 thus making it enforceable. Therefore, in the absence of any conflict it is possible to read the test of reasonable accommodation in employment contracts."

The Court further held, "A duty is, therefore, cast on the State to provide reasonable accommodation in the matter of employment subject to the burden of hardship test being satisfied. In the absence of a statutory definition of reasonable accommodation, the reasonable accommodation as set out in the protocol in the first instance can be considered. It will have to have a nexus with the financial burden on the institution and/or undertaking which will have to bear the burden and further the extent to which reasonable accommodation can be provided for."

The court incorporated the right to reasonable accommodation by declaring that "Reasonable accommodation, if read into Article 21, based on the U.N Protocol, would not be in conflict with municipal law. It would give added life and dimension to the ever-expanding concept of life and its true enjoyment."

Following this, the court concluded that the bank has a duty to provide reasonable accommodation to the petitioner subject to any undue burden. The court observed that no evidence was presented on how the financial burden would actually be a caused to the bank in providing reasonable accommodation to the petitioner even if it meant meeting his medical expenses. Consequently, the court allowed the petition and directed that the Petitioner be offered appointment and allowed to join the post.

Lalit and Others v Govt. of NCT and Another W.P. (C) No. 3444/2008

Judgement dated May 7, 2010 (Delhi High Court)

Hon'ble Mr. Justice Muralidhar of the Delhi High Court noted that the facts illustrated the lack of decent accommodation for children with disabilities and recognised the associated problems of lack of resources, hygiene and accountability in the running of institutions with disabled children.

The court held, "In the context of the inviolable human rights of the disabled, it is necessary to take note of the binding and mandatory provisions of the Persons with Disabilities (Equal Opportunities, Protection of Rights and Full Participation) Act, 1995 (specifically Sections 26 and 30) ('PDR Act') and the Convention on the Rights of Persons with Disabilities ('CRPD') which has been ratified by India. In particular, Article 7 which set out the obligations of the States towards children with disabilities, Article 9 which obliges the States to take appropriate measures to ensure access to "schools, housing, medical facilities', and Article 24 which deals with the right to education are relevant."

The court relied upon Article 24 of the CRPD which guaranteed the right to education and held that in the context of a disabled child housed in a state-run institution there are a cluster of laws all of which can be traced to the fundamental rights to liberty and a life with dignity. It held that in the context of a young person receiving education in a state-run institution as a resident scholar, the right to shelter and decent living is an inalienable facet of the right to education itself and when the State takes over the running of an educational institution that caters to the needs of the disabled, it has to account for the 'cascading effect' of multiple disadvantages that such children face.

In the context of the present case however, the court held that due to the limitation of resources, all the visually impaired persons at the Andh- Mahavidhyalala, irrespective of their age cannot possibly expect to be allowed to live there as the primary purpose should be to cater to the needs of young children studying up to class VIII. If this primary object was not kept in view, then it may result in an unfair denial of the right to education of other deserving young students who are visually challenged.

The court, thus directed the Respondent authorities to take every possible effort to see if all the 5 inmates who were given expulsion orders could be accommodated in any of the other institutions in Delhi. Sufficient time of 6 months should be given to them to make alternative arrangements and assistance should be given to help them find alternative accommodation. The court also observed that this case should act as a wakeup call for the government to monitor the functioning generally of all institutions under its control, particularly for the disabled. This case illustrates the incorporation of the CRPD principles with regard to reasonable accommodation and right to education of children. The court was called upon to balance the two rights, which it ultimately did by taking into account the level of disabilities faced by each group demanding accommodation.

The National Association for the Deaf v. Union of India
W.P.(C) No.6250/2010

Judgment dated November 24, 2011 (Delhi High Court)

This was a public interest petition filed by the National Association for the Deaf before the Delhi High Court on the non-availability of sign language interpreters in public services. The petition complained of the lack of availability of adequate number of sign language interpreters in various public places and sought for directions against the Ministry of Social Justice and Empowerment and other authorities to ensure access and better training of sign language interpreters.

While the court noted the lack of availability of sign language interpreters, it agreed with the Petitioner Association that due to non-availability of interpreters, the hearing impaired were unable to avail medical, transport and banking facilities and to also seek police help. With regard to the importance of ensuring the availability of support in the form of interpreters, the Court relied on the CRPD and held, "The United Nations Convention on the Rights of persons with disabilities adopted by the General Assembly and ratified by the Govt. of India on 1st October, 2007 also provides for taking appropriate measures to provide forms of live assistance and intermediaries including guides, readers and professional Sign Language Interpreters to facilitate accessibility to buildings and other facilities open to the public. Needless to state that all the said rights are composite part of life enshrined in Article 21 of the Constitution of India."

Based on this, the court issued specific directions to the respondent authorities which included undertaking a survey to assess the availability and requirements for sign language interpreters, appointing nodal officers to seek information from concerned authorities and prepare a report to be used for creation of new posts, creating courses and curricula for training of interpreters.

Bhagwan Dass and Anr. Vs. Punjab State Electricity Board (2003) 4 SCC 524

In this case, the Appellant was an Assistant Lineman in the Respondent Board. During his service, he became totally blind and the Respondent failed to accommodate him in an alternative post as per Section 47 of the PWD Act and terminated his service. Therefore, the appellant approached the High Court of Punjab and Haryana against the termination of his service. The high court dismissed the petition and the Appellant appealed to the Supreme Court.

The Supreme Court allowed the appeal relying on Section 47 of the PWD Act and observed that the Board had an obligation to follow this provision as the appellant had acquired disability during his service. On Section 47, the Court relied on a previous decision in Kunal Singh v. Union of India and Anr. (2003) 4 SCC 524 which held that, "In construing a provision of a social beneficial enactment that too dealing with disabled persons intended to give them equal opportunities, protection of rights and full participation, the view that advances the object of the Act and serves its purpose must be preferred to the one which obstructs the object and paralyses the purpose of the Act."

The court gave a broad interpretation to Section 47 and took a protective approach towards persons with disabilities by holding: "From the narrow point of view the officers were duty bound to follow the law and it was not open to them to allow their bias to defeat the lawful rights of the disabled employee. From the larger point of view the officers failed to realise that the disabled too are equal citizens of the country and have as much share in its resources as any other citizen. The denial of their rights would not only be unjust and unfair to them and their families but would create larger and graver problems for the society at large. What the law permits to them is no charity or largess but their right as equal citizens of the country."

Ritesh Sinha v. State of Haryana CWP NO. 3087 OF 2011 (Punjab and Haryana High Court)

In this case, an important interim order was passed by the High Court of Punjab and Haryana and the matter is still pending. The petitioner was a person with locomotor disability and was appointed as a clerk by the District and Sessions Judge, Karnal in the post reserved for physically disabled persons. Thereafter his services were terminated due to his inability to perform the duties as a clerk who was expected to write the office notes and maintain records in his own hands.

The court held that as the petitioner was well conversant with computer operations and that there could be plenty of work done by him like preparation of daily cause lists of all courts, certified copies of judgments, etc., which could be assigned to a computer savvy person like him. The court directed that in the interim, his dismissal order would remain stayed, and the respondents were directed to reinstate the petitioner in service with all benefits. The court even directed the respondents to immediately construct a ramp / slope so that the petitioner could enter his office and a compliance report to be submitted to court about the same. Further, it directed the respondents to see that a congenial atmosphere is created at the workplace so that the Petitioner is made an integral part of the mainstream workforce.

U.P. Vishesh Shikshak Association v. State of U.P. Misc Bench No. 5622/ 2010
Order dated June 17, 2010 (Allahabad High Court)

Here the Petitioner Association had filed a public interest petition before the Allahabad High Court contending that the pupil-teacher ratio so far as specialised teachers and children with disabilities was concerned was not adequate and claimed that the government circular on Integrated Education for Disabled Children Scheme mandated a pupil teacher ratio of 8:1. It also claimed that the Rehabilitation Council of India Act, 1992 imposed a statutory duty on the State to make arrangements for adequate number of teachers for persons with disabilities.

The Allahabad High Court recognised the statutory duty of the State to "provide all necessary help and assistance to physically disabled students. However, in response to an argument that orthopedically handicapped children do not require specialised teachers, it held, "We are of the view that now, the right to education and right to livelihood being the fundamental rights enshrined under Articles 21 and 21-A of the Constitution, the State Government has to make all efforts to provide necessary assistance to all disabled persons. Taking into consideration the meagre strength of 1291 teachers, we cannot presume that State Government may be able to impart education to disabled students."

Manjunatha v. Government of Karnataka and Ors. W.P. 35969/2010

Judgment dated September 29, 2011 (Karnataka High Court)

In this case, the petitioner, who was completely blind sought to apply for the B. Ed. Course under the government quota of seats in Karnataka. However, he was denied admission by reason of the condition that persons with disability greater than 75 per cent would not be eligible for admission. The announcement issued by the respondent permitted applications from persons with disability but restricted it to such applicants who had a disability exceeding 40 per cent but below 75 per cent.

The Karnataka High Court allowed the petition by holding that such a provision in the announcement ran counter to the PWD Act. The respondent government argued that the upper limit in the announcement was based on a similar provision in Karnataka Selection of Candidates for Admission to Teachers Certificate Higher Course (TCH) and Bachelor of Education Course (B.Ed.) Rules 1999 and therefore such a notification could not be challenged. The bench however, rejected this contention and held that even the Rules run contrary to the PWD Act and the state government could not rely on the Rules to deny admission to candidates having more than 75 per cent disability. The court ruled in favour of the petitioner and held that he was entitled to take up CET for admission to B.Ed. course and further declared that he shall not be denied admission on the basis of his disability exceeding 75 per cent. The observations of the court strengthened the protection for persons with disabilities as it effectively held that the disability legislations would take precedence over administrative rules of the government.

Kritika Purohit and Anr. v. State of Maharashtra and Ors. W.P. 979/2010, Bombay High Court

The petitioner was a visually impaired student who sought admission to the course in Bachelor of Physiotherapy but was not permitted to apply for the same. The petitioner contended that although the post of a physiotherapist was considered to be suitable for blind persons, the denial of courses in physiotherapy for blind persons ran counter to Section 39 of the PWD Act and that the respondents were obliged to make all accommodations for the Petitioner in conformity with Article 24(2) of the CRPD.

The respondents contended that it was not practical for the petitioner to be involved in the course. However, the court also noted the petitioner's reliance on the circular of the Mumbai University in mandating that resources should be made available to visually impaired student to allow them to complete their courses. In view of these materials, the court observed that the respondents had shown a negative attitude towards persons with disabilities and "have not cared to consider the object underlying the provisions of Disabilities Act, 1995."

Therefore, by an interim order dated August 2, 2010, it directed the Commissioner of Disabilities to consider all the materials and make suitable instructions to the respondents for making necessary arrangements for admission of visually challenged students. It also directed that the petitioner should be provisionally admitted for the course and should be provided with resources for translation of the material to braille.

Subsequently the court found that the petitioner had completed the first exam and had secured 62 per cent in the same. Therefore, it held that she should be allowed to be admitted and complete the course. However, the court noted that the state government had accepted the guidelines of the Maharashtra State Council for Occupational Therapy and Physiotherapy that visually impaired candidates are not fit for the physiotherapy course. On this, it noted the contentions of the Petitioner and also Xavier's Resource Centre for the Visually Challenged who claimed that a physiotherapist is not required to perform all the functions of physiotherapy and visually impaired physiotherapists can perform all functions with assistance if necessary.

They also pointed out various physiotherapists who were working in Maharashtra successfully for many years. The court held, "We are, therefore, of the view that the stand of the respondent authorities is clearly discriminatory and adversely affects the Right to Life and equal opportunities of the petitioner as also other such students similarly situated. The fact that petitioner though being visually impaired not only passed her first year examination with 62% marks and is successfully studying in 2nd year, and several visually impaired persons have been working as professional physiotherapists in India as well as abroad appeals to us not to allow the petitioner as also others in the same position to be discriminated against or disqualified on that ground."

Thus, the court stayed the decision of the state government and directed the respondents to consider candidates with visual disability for admission to the course in physiotherapy.

Chapter 5

International Developments in Disability Rights

The global human rights framework has steadily evolved to address the rights of vulnerable populations, including persons with disabilities. The Universal Declaration of Human Rights provided the initial foundation, followed by legally binding treaties like the International Covenants on Civil and Political Rights and on Economic, Social and Cultural Rights. Subsequent conventions focused on protecting the rights of specific groups, such as racial minorities, women, and children.

In response to the human rights challenges faced by people with disabilities, the United Nations has initiated a range of agreements, statements, and international conferences. This has led to a gradual shift towards a human rights perspective on disability, with 39 countries enacting non-discrimination or equal opportunity legislation.

A landmark development was the adoption of the World Programme of Action Concerning Disabled Persons in 1982, during the International Year of Disabled Persons. The Programme emphasized equal opportunity and access rights for people with disabilities, recognizing the relationship between disability and the environment. It called on governments to establish legal frameworks, eliminate barriers, and support the growth of disabled persons' organizations to achieve these objectives.

The UN Decade of Disabled Persons from 1983 to 1992 was declared to provide a timeframe for states to implement the World Programme of Action. This signaled a concerted global effort to advance the rights and inclusion of persons with disabilities through policy and legislative measures.

The UN Standard Rules on the Equalization of Opportunities for Persons with Disabilities, 1994

The United Nations' endorsement of a human rights approach to disability is evident in the Standard Rules on the Equalization of Opportunities for Persons with Disabilities, adopted by the UN General Assembly in 1993. The Rules focus on empowering individuals with disabilities and increasing structural access, as a direct outcome of the rights-based philosophy established through the World Programme of Action and the Decade of Disabled Persons.

The Special Rapporteur on Disability oversees the implementation of the Standard Rules, reporting that they are now being applied globally by governments and disability organizations for advocacy, policy-making, legislation, and evaluation.

The 22 Rules are divided into four chapters addressing: preconditions for equal participation; target areas for equal participation, such as accessibility, education, employment, and culture; implementation measures, including policy-making, legislation, and government systems; and a monitoring mechanism.

The Rules reflect a strong human rights perspective, placing the responsibility on states to remove obstacles to the full exercise of rights and obligations by children and adults with disabilities, in partnership with individuals and organizations. Initially non-binding, the Standard Rules have gained increased authority with a recent UN resolution, suggesting governments are now legally required to adhere to them. This represents a significant advancement in the global commitment to enabling the human rights of persons with disabilities through the equalization of opportunities.

Resolutions of the United Nations Commission on Human Rights

The United Nations has made significant strides in affirming disability as a human rights issue. In 1998, the UN Commission on Human Rights passed resolution 1998/31, recognizing the UN's responsibility for the human rights of people with disabilities and declaring that inequality and discrimination related to disability are violations of human rights.

Building on this, in 2000 the Commission adopted a new resolution that reaffirmed the 1998 resolution and stated that any violation of the Standard Rules on the Equalization of Opportunities for Persons with Disabilities is an infringement of the human rights of persons with disabilities. This can be interpreted as the establishment of an international norm, requiring all nations to adhere to the Standard Rules.

The 2000 resolution also expressed an urgent need for action, inviting the High Commissioner for Human Rights and the Special Rapporteur on Disability to examine measures to strengthen the protection and monitoring of the human rights of persons with disabilities. These resolutions represent a significant breakthrough in the global shift towards a human rights approach to disability, firmly embedding the responsibility of states to uphold the rights and equal opportunities of people with disabilities. The Commission's actions have elevated disability from a welfare or medical issue to a matter of fundamental human rights.

Regional Agreements and Declarations

The Inter-American Convention for the Elimination of All Forms of Discrimination against Persons with Disabilities is a groundbreaking international treaty solely focused on the rights of people with disabilities. Adopted in 1999 and entering into force in 2001, the Convention is open for ratification by member states of the Organization of American States.

The Convention defines disability broadly, as a physical, mental, or sensory impairment, whether permanent or temporary, that limits the capacity to perform essential daily activities and can be caused or exacerbated by the economic and social environment. Governments are required to implement measures in legislation, social programs, education, and employment to fully integrate people with disabilities into society.

Central to the Convention's aims are provisions for rehabilitation, education, job training, and other measures to promote the independence and quality of life of people with disabilities. Regional organizations have also played a pivotal role in drawing attention to disability issues and driving action. In 1992, the Economic and Social Commission for Asia and the Pacific (ESCAP) declared the 1993-2002 period as the Asian and Pacific Decade of Disabled Persons. Governments in the region committed to the full participation and equality of people with disabilities through the Proclamation and Agenda for Action.

The focus during the Decade was on expanding opportunities for the full participation and equality of people with disabilities in the development process, as well as improving public awareness and increasing accessibility and communication.

Disabled Persons International (DPI) Sapporo Declaration, 2002

The disability community has been instrumental in promoting a rights-based approach to disability, advocating for the establishment of a dedicated international convention focused on the rights of individuals with disabilities. Disabled Persons International (DPI), a global network representing people with disabilities, issued the Sapporo Declaration in October 2002 following a conference that brought together delegates from 109 countries. This declaration highlights the need for comprehensive human rights protections encompassing civil, political, economic, social, and cultural rights, along with a robust monitoring mechanism that incorporates the perspectives of individuals with disabilities. International disability conferences stress the importance of equality, inclusion, and specific priorities such as education, enhancing quality of life, combating discrimination, addressing barriers, and providing necessary resources to ensure the full participation of individuals with disabilities in society.

International Norms and Standards Relating to Disability

In recent years, the United Nations has organized three significant gatherings of experts to deliberate on global standards and norms pertaining to disability. The initial meeting took place in Berkeley, California in 1998, gathering fifteen experts in international law and disability policy. Their conversations centered on strategies to enhance awareness of international norms and standards related to disability within domestic laws and policies. The group also worked on developing suitable legislative frameworks and model national laws to support the implementation of international norms and standards. At the global level, the experts proposed two key approaches to advancing the rights of individuals with disabilities: leveraging existing UN human rights mechanisms to uphold the human rights of individuals with disabilities and establishing a new international human rights instrument specific to disability issues. Notably, the right to inclusive education and the engagement of individuals with disabilities in policymaking and decision-making processes were given special attention. A subsequent international seminar, led by the UN Special Rapporteur on Disability, was held in Stockholm, Sweden in November 2000. In this seminar, 27 experts crafted guidelines to enhance the identification and reporting of violations of the rights of individuals with disabilities, underscoring the importance of bringing attention to these human rights infringements on a global platform. The experts recommended data collection in five key areas: individual cases, legal proceedings, legislation, media coverage, and government initiatives, services, and practices. This comprehensive focus was expected to offer a more comprehensive understanding of the human rights landscape for individuals with disabilities.

Global estimates from the World Health Organization suggest that approximately 15% of the world's population experiences some form of disability, with over 80% of these individuals residing in nations classified as Low- or Middle-Income. India, home to a population exceeding 1.36 billion, reports that more than 2.2% of its citizens grapple with severe mental or physical impairments. In our current progressive era, which emphasizes the integration and inclusion of all individuals as a cornerstone of sustainable progress, it has become increasingly crucial to implement targeted initiatives addressing the health and welfare of those living with disabilities.

It's important to note that disability is not a fixed state but rather a fluid condition, making it challenging to establish a universally accepted definition of what constitutes a disability or who qualifies as disabled. In India, the criteria for categorizing individuals as disabled underwent a significant revision in 2016 with the introduction of the Rights of People with Disabilities act (RPwD). This legislation established a comprehensive list encompassing 21 distinct disability categories. The 2021 Census incorporated this updated definition, which notably expanded to recognize physical deformities and injuries resulting from acid attacks as disabilities. This inclusion entitles affected individuals to various forms of government assistance and support programs.

Official data on the number of individuals with disabilities in India, derived from the most recent Population Census and comprehensive surveys conducted by the National Sample Survey Organisation, indicated approximately 21 million people (roughly 2% of the population) at the turn of the millennium. However, estimates vary across different sources. A recent World Bank report on disability in India suggests that emerging evidence points to a higher prevalence, with disabled persons potentially comprising between 5% and 8% of the Indian population (approximately 55-90 million individuals).

There is widespread concern that people with disabilities are among the most marginalized groups in India's development process. To formulate effective and efficient policy interventions aimed at improving the lives of disabled individuals, it is crucial to gain a clear understanding of the scope and nature of disability in the country. While the government and public sector must play a pivotal role in this effort, it may be neither feasible nor desirable for them to shoulder the entire responsibility.

Moreover, the situations and policy needs of various groups of disabled persons in India are highly diverse. Significant differences exist in societal attitudes towards different types of disabilities, further complicated by variations based on gender, socioeconomic class, and place of residence (rural or urban).

The Population Census and NSS surveys serve as the two primary sources of official statistics in India. However, these sources differ considerably in their overall estimates of individuals with various types of disabilities and their composition. These discrepancies largely stem from differences in concepts, definitions, and data collection methodologies. Consequently, this section will address the dimensions of disability as reflected by these two sources separately.

Chapter 6

Findings, Suggestions and Conclusion

After the elaborate study of various aspects of disability and their impact upon the socio economic level of the persons with disabilities, a well deserved finding can be reached that there is an overall imminent need to take care of persons with disabilities in a sensible manner. The approach requires to be shifted from mere sympathy to that of companionship by the sensible members of the society. The disability need not be taken as a noun but rather as a mere adjective and the person with a disability needs to be seen beyond his disability also. For removing the disability, adequate legal measures are warranted which can smoothen the life of any person with disability. The present problem of lack of access of public offices and transport be removed with immediate effect adequate support mechanism be ensured for the meeting of minimum and basic level of financial security for the persons with disabilities depending their level of disabilities. At the first instance, the persons with natural disabilities should be identified at the time of their birth and a policy and support for the education, vocation training and the rehabilitation of that disabled persons should be planned and undertaken by a particular department. In other cases, where disability is not natural and is a result of one or the other factors at the different ages of the life of the person, he should be identified as soon as the disability creeps in the life of person and then depending upon the type and level of his disability, adequate support measures should be undertaken. Besides that a fund for meeting the disability complications as well as the medical ailments of the disabled should be established for meeting the probable and possible unavoidable complications of the persons with disability. At the level of society, workshop and seminars be conducted at the school, colleges, and public offices and at the National media level to sensitize the public, the abled ones about the special needs, temperaments and requirements of the persons with disabilities. Once the person with disability comes of age and has been rehabilitated in life after his vocational training, a suitable match is arranged with another person of disability from the other sex, which can complement the life of both the persons with disabilities, if a normal match is not possible at all. Special security measures ensuring the social security of the persons with disability are taken for avoiding the old age multiplication of problems of the disabled during their old age. A community living programme supported by State or non state actors like NGOs be initialed by planning and constructing community halls with special attention to the needs of the different sections of the disabled.

The real issue behind these barriers is the disability insensitive attitude of the society. Even a stringent law can do very less unless there is a change in the mindset of people and a willingness to accept and respect disabled people. There is an attitude of relating a disabled person with his or her disability and not to his/her abilities. The society should be dynamic enough to accept all differences, as the world exists only because of its differences and the natural balance among them. It also becomes the duty of each member of the society to respect Individuality and Mutual Rights of any (disabled) member of the society. The society should develop a natural tendency to provide Equal Opportunities to disabled people, whereby they can enjoy their rights and as well contribute to the society. All citizens should have the attitude to Value the Contribution of disabled people as they do their own. For such an attitudinal shift to happen the society should believe in Disabled people and that they are like anybody else.

Least priority has been given to the education of disabled children, due to the following reasons: The attitude of the parents, family members and the community is that, there is no use of a disabled child being educated and it is a wastage of time, money and other resources, as they think that a disabled child is not productive in any way. The capitalist mentality of the society also prevents the disabled child from enjoying the Right to Education as conferred by the Constitution of India.

When there are other siblings for a disabled child, the disabled child gets the least priority in education compared to his/her siblings, either due to poverty of parents or the attitudinal barriers in the society. Poverty and Disability is a vicious circle. Due to poverty education is denied for children. Even if parents from the economically weaker sections of the society want to educate their children, the opportunity of a disabled child going to school is a rarity, as the cost involved in educating a disabled child is more when compared to a non- disabled child, due to the architectural barriers in the society.

The prevalence of architectural and environmental barriers such as inaccessible built environment, school buildings, roads, transport and so on. Many times parents will have to carry their disabled child due to these barriers. They cannot use public transport and private transport is too expensive for them. The education system is also inaccessible for many disabled students, as the teaching methods, learning aids, the curriculum itself and the evaluation system is not disabled friendly. (Braille books and materials, readers for students with visual impairment, sign language interpretation and teaching are not available in most schools). Even when alternative teaching methods are used, the same methods are not used for evaluation. Sarva Shiksha Abhiyaan (SSA) talks of Education for all. The fact remains that many disabled people are not enrolled under this scheme due to the severity of Disability. Also, teachers are not trained in inclusive education.

The Persons with Disabilities Act, 1995 does not speak of reservations in Higher Educational Institutions and only talks about open universities. Many Disabled People are denied entry into professional courses like MBA, Engineering and Medicine due to their disability.

There is a lot that can be done to change this, including better education; ensuring there are more opportunities for disabled people and people who aren't disabled to have positive interactions; and encouraging more positive portrayals of disability and disabled people in the media.

Despite the barriers people with disabilities face, the Internet has been viewed as having incredible potential related to promoting social inclusion of people with disabilities. People with disabilities who were able to access and use the Internet were reporting noticeably larger benefits from it. It has largely improved the quality of their lives, made them better informed about the world, helped them meet people with similar interests and experiences and gave them more connections to the world than the general population. It seems a great boon to them to make their life more challenging. They feel more confident and self-reliant.

However, despite important advances at National and International level, and International Day of Disabled Persons (December 3rd), all acknowledge integration as an issue of social change: changes in legislation, policy and awareness of disability as a human rights issue. Most of the persons with disabilities in India are unaware of their rights. There is need to a sensitization programme about the rights of disabled as on today when they have to undergo lots of hurdles because of the lack of trained professionals to issue the certificate, and lack of standardized tools available to identify them in the different languages.

Disabled people can change their lot in society through their increased participation, their skills, experience and insights as well as the attitude of the society which they have successfully done in some countries; the situation for the vast majority of the world's disabled people remains bleak.

Some Facts About Disability

- In some countries, 90 per cent of disabled children will not survive beyond the age of 20; 90 per cent of intellectually impaired children do not survive beyond the age of five.
- 98 per cent of disabled people in developing countries are totally neglected.
- Most people with spinal cord injuries in the developing world die within two years of injury due to lack of facilities.

- The majority of countries have no free medical care or social security system.
- In the US, Canada and UK, 60 per cent of disabled people live below the poverty line.
- In developing countries, disabled children are unlikely to get an education or find ajob.
- In the developed world, the majority of disabled children receive segregated, underachieving education and are twice as likely to be unemployed when they grow up.
- 80 per cent of disabled people live in Asia and the Pacific but they receive just 2 per cent of resources allocated to disabled people.
- Citing Census 2011, the report states that there are 26.8 million persons with disabilities in India, making up 2.21 per cent of the total population.
- There are 14.9 million males and 11.9 million females with disabilities in India – accounting for 56 and 44 per cent of the total population of disabled persons. About 2.41 per cent of India's male population and 2.01 per cent of its female population reports having a disability.
- As many as 18 million persons with disabilities (69 per cent of the disabled population) live in rural India, and about eight million (31 per cent) live in urban areas.
- Roughly 2.45 per cent of persons with disabilities in India are from Scheduled Castes (SCs) and 2.05 per cent are from Scheduled Tribes (STs).
- The report presents data on the number of persons with different kinds of disabilities in the country. It says that 20 per cent of persons with disabilities report impairments in movement, 19 per cent face disability in seeing, 19 per cent in hearing, and seven per cent in speech. The report notes that six per cent of the disabled population faces 'mental retardation' or intellectual disability which results in difficulty in understanding, comprehension or communication.
- Over a fifth of all persons with disabilities in India are elderly persons, or those above 60 years of age.

- According to Census 2011 data, 61 per cent of children with disabilities (aged 5-19 years) are in an educational institution, 12 per cent have been in such institutions in the past, and 27 per cent have never attended one. The report states that 50 per cent of children with mental disabilities have never attended any educational institution.

- Citing Census 2011, the report notes that nearly a third of all persons with disabilities in India are working. This is the case for 47 per cent of the male and 23 per cent of the female disabled population. Among women with disabilities, 25 per cent of those in rural India, and 16 per cent of those in urban areas, are working.

- About 1.46 crore persons with disabilities are literate, accounting for 54.4 per cent of the disabled population. At 70.8 per cent, Kerala has the highest literacy rate among disabled persons, while Arunachal Pradesh has the lowest at 38.8 per cent.

- Nearly half of the total disabled population in the country live in one of the following five states: Uttar Pradesh (15.5 per cent), Maharashtra (11.05 per cent), Bihar (8.69 per cent), Andhra Pradesh (8.45 per cent) and West Bengal (7.52 per cent).

- More than 50 per cent of children with disabilities aged less than six live in one of these four states: Uttar Pradesh (20.31 per cent), Bihar (14.24 per cent), Maharashtra (10.64 per cent) and West Bengal (6.48 per cent).

- At 2.98 per cent, Sikkim has the highest prevalence of persons with disabilities among all states and union territories, while Daman and Diu has the lowest (0.9 per cent).

- The state of Bihar has the highest proportion of children under six in its disabled population, at 12.48 per cent. Kerala has the lowest proportion of children under six with disabilities at 3.44 per cent.

- The report states that 22.4 per cent of the disabled population in rural areas, and 19.9 per cent in urban areas, reported receiving aid or help from the government.

- India's Constitution enshrines the principles of "equality, freedom, justice and dignity" for all citizens. Recognizing the need for focused attention on disability-related policy issues, the Ministry of Social Justice and Empowerment established the Department of Empowerment of Persons with Disabilities (Divyangjan) in May 2012. This department works to advance the empowerment of individuals with disabilities.

- The Indian government has launched several key initiatives to support the welfare of disabled persons. One such program is the Deendayal Disabled Rehabilitation Scheme, which provides financial support to non-governmental organizations for projects aimed at rehabilitating persons with disabilities and related endeavors.

- The National Health Profile 2020 report indicates that approximately 2.7% of India's population, or around 35 million individuals, live with a disability. Visual impairment, hearing impairment, and orthopedic impairment are the most prevalent types of disabilities in the country. However, a recent World Health Organization (WHO) report suggests a higher prevalence, estimating that 15% of India's population experiences some form of disability. The WHO report also highlights a significant disparity in access to healthcare and social services for this demographic.

- In response to these challenges, the Indian government has implemented various measures to promote disability inclusion and accessibility. A notable example is the Rights of Persons with Disabilities Act, 2016, which aims to safeguard the rights and improve the lives of individuals with disabilities across the nation. Programmes/initiatives for Disabled in India

- **Accessible India Campaign: Creation of Accessible Environment for PwDs:** A nation-wide flagship campaign for achieving universal accessibility that will enable persons with disabilities to gain access for equal opportunity and live independently and participate fully in all aspects of life in an inclusive society. The campaign targets at enhancing the accessibility of built environment, transport system and Information & communication ecosystem.

- **DeenDayal Disabled Rehabilitation Scheme: Under the scheme financial assistance is provided to NGOs for providing various services to Persons with Disabilities, like special schools, vocational training centres, community based rehabilitation, pre-school and early intervention etc**
- **Assistance to Disabled Persons for Purchase / fitting of Aids and Appliances (ADIP): The Scheme aims at helping the disabled persons by bringing suitable, durable, scientifically-manufactured, modern, standard aids and appliances within their reach.**
- **National Fellowship for Students with Disabilities (RGMF)**
- The scheme aims to increase opportunities to students with disabilities for pursuing higher education. Under the Scheme, 200 Fellowships per year are granted to students with disability.
- **Schemes of the National Trust** for the Welfare of Persons with Autism, Cerebral Palsy, Mental Retardation and Multiple Disabilities.

Issues and Challenges

- **Health:** A large number of disabilities are preventable, including those arising from medical issues during birth, maternal conditions, malnutrition, as well as accidents and injuries. However, the health sector especially in rural India has failed to react proactively to disability. Further there are lack of affordable access to proper health care, aids and appliances. Healthcare facilities and poorly trained health-workers in rehabilitation centres is another concern.
- **Education:** The education system is not inclusive. Inclusion of children with mild to moderate disabilities in regular schools has remained a major challenge. There are various issues such as availability special schools, access to schools, trained teachers, and availability of educational materials for the disabled. Further, reservations for the disabled in higher educational institutions has not been fulfilled in many instances

- **Employment:** Even though many disabled adults are capable of productive work, disabled adults have far lower employment rates than the general population. The situation is even worse in the private sector, where much less disabled are employed
- **Accessibility: Physical accessibility in buildings, transportation, access to services etc still remain a major challenge.**
- **Discrimination/Social Exclusion:** Negative attitudes held by the families of the disabled, and often the disabled themselves, hinder disabled persons from taking an active part in the family, community or workforce. Differently-abled people face discrimination in everyday life. People suffering from mental illness or mental retardation face the worst stigma and are subject to severe social exclusion.
- **Inadequate data and statistics:** The lack of rigorous and comparable data and statics further hinders inclusion of persons with disabilities. The major issues with collection of data and measuring disability are: Difficult to define disability, Coverage: Different purposes require different disability data, Reluctance in reporting disability as disability is considered to be a stigma in many places/societies
- **Poor implementation of policies and schemes hinders the inclusion of disabled persons. Though various acts and schemes have been laid down with an aim to empower the disabled, their enforcement face many challenges.**
- **Prevention:** Preventive health programs need to be strengthened and all children need to be screened at a young age. Kerala has already started an early prevention programme. Comprehensive Newborn Screening (CNS) programme seeks early identification of deficits in infants and reduce the state's burden of disability.
- **Awareness:** People with disabilities need to be better integrated into society by overcoming stigma. There should be awareness campaigns to educate and aware people about different kinds of disability. Success stories of people with disabilities can be showcased to inculcate positive attitude among people

- **Employment:** Disabled adults need to be empowered with employable skills The private sector needs to be encouraged to employ them.
- **Better measurement: The scale of disability in India needs to be better understood by improving the measurement of disability.**
- **Education:** State-wise strategies on education for children with special needs need to be devised. There should be proper teacher training to address the needs of differently-abled children and facilitate their inclusion in regular schools. Further there should be more special schools and ensure educational material for differently-abled children
- **Access:** Safety measures like road safety, safety in residential areas, public transport system etc, should be taken up. Further, it should be made legally binding to make buildings disabled-friendly
- **Policy Interventions:** More budgetary allocation for welfare of the disabled. There should be a disability budgeting on line of gender budget. Proper implementation of schemes should be ensured. There should be proper monitoring mechanisms and accountability of public funds.

Need of the Hour

As disability has become a human rights and equal opportunities issue, society at all levels requires training to understand the reality of disabled people's lives from this new perspective. Disability should be considered as an important issue by the Government so that their problem can be tackled in the community. The services should cover all types of disabled who need rehabilitation services and it should be part of mainstream development in the community. A multi-sectoral approach including social integration interventions, health, education, and vocational programs are important issues related to rehabilitation services. Primary health care system must play a major role both as a provider and supporter, and should engage with initiatives such as early identification of impairments and providing basic interventions, referrals to specialized services such as physical, occupational, and speech therapies, prosthetics and orthotics, and corrective surgeries. The educational sector should be more inclusive by adapting newer techniques with respect to content of the curriculum, methods of teaching and ensuring that classrooms, facilities, and educational materials more accessible. Children with multiple or severe disabilities who might require extensive additional support may access education through the use of innovative methods best suited to their context. Collaboration with the employment and labor sectors is essential to ensure that both youth and adults with disabilities have access to training and work opportunities at community level.

In addition to mainstream services, some people with disabilities may require access to specific measures, support services, or training. In this process, involvement of persons with disability is of paramount importance as they give insight into their problems and suggest possible solution. Human resource capacity can be improved through effective education, training, and recruitment. A review of the knowledge and competence of staff in relevant areas can provide a starting point for developing appropriate measures to improve them. Manpower generation by promoting new courses and initiating degree and diploma courses like Physical Medicine and Rehabilitation will address the problem of shortage of manpower in long run. Focus on educating disabled children as close to the main stream as possible. Increase public awareness and understanding of disability. Governments, voluntary organizations, and professional associations should consider running social marketing campaigns that change attitudes on stigmatized issues such as HIV, mental illness, and leprosy. Involving the media is vital to the success of these campaigns and to ensuring the dissemination of positive stories about persons with disabilities and their families. Generating representative community-based data will help to plan and execute appropriate measures to address the problems of persons living with disability. Research is essential for increasing public understanding about disability issues, informing disability policy and programmes, and efficiently allocating resources. Some of the important areas of research can be quality of life and well-being of people with disabilities; barriers to mainstream and specific services, and what works in overcoming them in different contexts; accessibility and universal design programmes appropriate for low-income-settings.

National Policy for Persons with Disabilities

The Constitution of India ensures equality, freedom, justice and dignity of all individuals and implicitly mandates an inclusive society for all including persons with disabilities. In the recent years, there have been vast and positive changes in the perception of the society towards persons with disabilities. It has been realized that a majority of persons with disabilities can lead a better quality of life if they have equal opportunities and effective access to rehabilitation measures.

2. According to the Census 2001, there are 2.19 crore persons with disabilities in India who constitute 2.13 percent of the total population. This includes persons with visual, hearing, speech, locomotor and mental disabilities. Seventy five per cent of persons with disabilities live in rural areas, 49 per cent of disabled population is literate and only 34 per cent are employed. The earlier emphasis on medical rehabilitation has now been replaced by an emphasis on social rehabilitation. There has been an increasing recognition of abilities of persons with disabilities and emphasis on mainstreaming them in the society based on their capabilities. The Government of India has enacted three legislations for persons with disabilities viz.

Persons with Disability (Equal Opportunities, Protection of Rights and Full Participation) Act, 1995, which provides for education, employment, creation of barrier free environment, social security, etc.

National Trust for Welfare of Persons with Autism, Cerebral Palsy, Mental Retardation and Multiple Disability Act, 1999 has provisions for legal guardianship of the four categories and creation of enabling environment for as much independent living as possible.

Rehabilitation Council of India Act, 1992 deals with the development of manpower for providing rehabilitation services.

3. In addition to the legal framework, extensive infrastructure has been developed. The following seven national Institutes are working for development of manpower in different areas, namely, Institute for the Physically Handicapped, New Delhi.

National Institute of Visually Handicapped, Dehradun

National Institute for Orthopaedically Handicapped, Kolkata

National Institute for Mentally Handicapped, Secunderabad.

National Institute for Hearing Handicapped, Mumbai

National Institute of Rehabilitation Training & Research, Cuttack.

National Institute for Empowerment of Persons with Multiple Disabilities, Chennai.

4. There are five Composite Rehabilitation Centres, four Regional Rehabilitation Centres and 120 District Disability Rehabilitation Centres (DDRCs) providing various kinds of rehabilitation services to persons with disabilities. There are also several national institutions under the Ministry of Health & Family Welfare working in the field of rehabilitation, like National Institute of Mental Health and Neuro Sciences, Bangalore; All India Institute of Physical Medicine and Rehabilitation, Mumbai; All India Institute of Speech and Hearing, Mysore; Central Institute of Psychiatry, Ranchi, etc. In addition, certain State Government institutions also provide rehabilitation services. Besides, 250 private institutions conduct training courses for rehabilitation professionals.

5. National Handicapped and Finance Development Corporation (NHFDC) has been providing loans on concessional terms for undertaking self-employment ventures by the persons with disabilities through State Channelizing Agencies.

6. Panchayati Raj Institutions at Village level, Intermediary level and District level have been entrusted with the welfare of persons with disabilities.

7. India is a signatory to the Declaration on the Full Participation and Equality of People with Disabilities in the Asia Pacific Region. India is also a signatory to the Biwako Millennium Framework for action towards an inclusive, barrier free and rights based society. India is currently participating in the negotiations on the UN Convention on Protection and Promotion of the Rights and Dignity of Persons with Disabilities.

National Policy Statement

8. The National Policy recognizes that Persons with Disabilities are valuable human resource for the country and seeks to create an environment that provides them equal opportunities, protection of their rights and full participation in society. The focus of the policy shall be on the following:

I. Prevention of Disabilities

9. Since disability, in a large number of cases, is preventable, there will be strong emphasis on prevention of disabilities. Programme for prevention of diseases, which result in disability and the creation of awareness regarding measures to be taken for prevention of disabilities during the period of pregnancy and thereafter will be intensified and their coverage expanded.

II. Rehabilitation Measures

10. Rehabilitation measures can be classified into three distinct groups:
   - physical rehabilitation, which includes early detection and intervention, counseling & medical interventions and provision of aids & appliances. It will also include the development of rehabilitation professionals.
   - educational rehabilitation including vocational education and
   - economic rehabilitation for a dignified life in society.

II A. Physical Rehabilitation Strategies

(a) Early Detection and Intervention

11. Early detection of disability and intervention through drug or non-drug therapies helps in minimization of impact of disability. Therefore, there will be emphasis on early detection and early intervention, and necessary facilities will be created towards this end. Government will take measures to disseminate information regarding availability of such facilities to the people especially in rural areas.

(b) Counseling & Medical Rehabilitation

12. Physical rehabilitation measures including counseling, strengthening capacities of persons with disabilities and their families, physiotherapy, occupational therapy, psychotherapy, surgical correction and intervention, vision assessment, vision stimulation, speech therapy, audiological rehabilitation and special education shall be extended to cover all the districts in the country by active involvement and participation of State Governments, local level institutions, NGOs including associations of parents and persons with disabilities.

13. Currently, rehabilitation services are largely available in and around urban areas. Since seventy five percent persons with disabilities live in rural areas, the services run by professionals will be extended to cover uncovered and un-served areas. Privately owned rehabilitation service centres shall be regulated for maintenance of minimum standards which shall be laid down.

14. To expand coverage in rural and unserved areas, new District Disability Rehabilitation Centres (DDRCs) will be set up with support from the State Government.

15. The National Rural Health Mission through Accredited Social Health Activist (ASHA) addresses the health needs of rural population, especially the vulnerable sections of society. The ASHA inter-alia will take care of the comprehensive services to the persons with disabilities at the grass root level.

(c) Assistive Devices

16. The Government of India has been assisting persons with disabilities in procuring durable and scientifically manufactured, modern aids and appliances of ISI standard that can promote their physical, social and psychological independence by reducing the effect of disabilities.

17. Every year through National Institutes, State Governments, DDRCs and NGOs, persons with disabilities are provided with devices such as prostheses and orthoses, tricycles, wheel chair, surgical footwear and devices for activities of daily living, learning equipments (Braille writing equipments, Dictaphone, CD player/ tape recorder), low vision aids, special mobility aids like canes for blind, hearing aids, educational kits, communication aids, assistive & alerting devices and devices suitable for the persons with mental disabilities. The availability of devices will be expanded to cover uncovered and under-serviced areas.

18. Private, public and joint sector enterprises involved in the manufacture of high tech assistive devices for persons with disabilities will be provided financial support by the public sector banks.

(d) Development of Rehabilitation Professionals

19. Human resource requirements for rehabilitation of persons with disabilities will be assessed and development plan will be prepared so that the rehabilitation strategies do not suffer from lack of manpower.

II B. Education for Persons with Disabilities

20. Education is the most effective vehicle of social and economic empowerment. In keeping with the spirit of the Article 21A of the Constitution guaranteeing education as a fundamental right and Section 26 of the Persons with Disabilities Act, 1995, free and compulsory education has to be provided to all children with disabilities up to the minimum age of 18 years. According

to the Census, 2001, fifty-one percent persons with disabilities are illiterate. This is a very large percentage. There is a need for mainstreaming of the persons with disabilities in the general education system through Inclusive education.

21. Sarva Shiksha Abhiyan (SSA) launched by the Government has the goal of eight years of elementary schooling for all children including children with disabilities in the age group of 6-14 years by 2010. Children with disabilities in the age group of 15-18 years are provided free education under Integrated Education for Disabled Children (IEDC) Scheme.

22. Under SSA, a continuum of educational options, learning aids and tools, mobility assistance, support services etc. are being made available to students with disabilities. This includes education through an open learning system and open schools, alternative schooling, distance education, special schools, wherever necessary home based education, itinerant teacher model, remedial teaching, part time classes, Community Based Rehabilitation (CBR) and vocational education.

23. IEDC Scheme implemented through the State Governments, Autonomous Bodies and Voluntary Organizations provides hundred percent financial assistance for various facilities like special teachers, books and stationery, uniform, transport, readers allowance for the visually handicapped, hostel allowance, equipment cost, removal/ modification of architectural barriers, financial assistance for purchase/ production of instructional material, training of general teachers and equipment for resource rooms.

24. There will be concerted effort on the part of the Government to improve identification of children with disabilities through regular surveys, their enrollment in appropriate schools and their continuation till they successfully complete their education. The Government will endeavor to provide right kind of learning material and books to the children with disabilities, suitably trained and sensitized teachers and schools which are accessible and disabled friendly.

25. Government of India is providing scholarships to students with disabilities for pursuing studies at post school level. Government will continue to support the scholarships and expand its coverage.

26. Facilities for technical and vocational education designed to inculcate and bolster skill development suited to various types of productive activities by adaptation of the existing institutes or accelerated setting up of institutes in un-served / underserved areas will be encouraged. NGOs will also be encouraged to provide vocational training.

27. Persons with disabilities will be provided access to the Universities, technical institutions and other institutions of higher learning to pursue higher and professional courses.

II C. Economic Rehabilitation of Persons with Disabilities

28. Economic rehabilitation of Persons with disabilities comprise of both wage employment in organized sector and self-employment. Supporting structure of services by way of vocational rehabilitation centres and vocational training centres will be developed to ensure that disabled persons in both urban and rural areas have increased opportunities for productive and gainful employment. Strategies for economic empowerment of persons with disabilities would be the following.

(i) Employment in Government Establishments

The PWD Act, 1995 provides for 3% reservation in employment in the establishments of Government of India and Public Sector Undertakings (PSUs) against identified posts. The status of reservation for Government in various Ministries / Departments against identified posts in Group A, B, C & D is 3.07%, 4.41%, 3.76% and 3.18% respectively. In PSUs, the reservation status in Group A, B, C & D is 2.78%, 8.54%, 5.04% and 6.75%, respectively. Government will ensure reservation in identified posts in the Government sector including public sector undertakings in accordance with the provisions of the PWD Act, 1995. The list of identified posts, which was notified in 2001, will be reviewed and updated.

(ii) Wage employment in Private sector

Development of appropriate skills in persons with disabilities will be encouraged for their employability in private sector. Vocational rehabilitation and training Centres engaged in developing appropriate skills amongst persons with disabilities keeping in view their potential and abilities will be encouraged to expand their services. Considering rapid growth of employment opportunities in service sector, persons with disabilities will be encouraged to undertake skill training suitable to the market requirement. Pro-active measures like incentives, awards, tax exemptions etc. will be taken to encourage the employment of persons with disabilities in the private sector.

(iii) Self-employment

Considering slow pace of growth in employment opportunities in the organized sector, self-employment of persons with disabilities will be promoted. This will be done through vocational education and management training. Further, the existing system of providing loans at softer terms from the NHFDC will be improved to make it easily accessible with transparent and efficient procedures of processing. The Government will also encourage self-employment by providing incentives, tax concessions, exemptions from duties, preferential treatment for procurement of goods and services by the Government from the enterprises of persons with disabilities, etc. Priority in financial support will be given to Self Help Groups formed by the persons with disabilities.

III. Women with disabilities

29. According to Census-2001, there are 93.01 lakh women with disabilities, which constitute 42.46 percent of total disabled population. Women with disabilities require protection against exploitation and abuse. Special programmes will be developed for education, employment and providing of other rehabilitation services to women with disabilities keeping in view their special

needs. Special educational and vocation training facilities will be setup. Programmes will be undertaken to rehabilitate abandoned disabled women/ girls by encouraging their adoption in families, support to house them and impart them training for gainful employment skills. The Government will encourage the projects where representation of women with disabilities is ensured at least to the extent of twenty five percent of total beneficiaries.

30. Steps shall be taken to provide short duration stay homes for women with disabilities, hostels for working disabled women, and homes for aged disabled women.

31. It has been noted that women with disabilities have serious difficulty in looking after their children. The Government will take up a programme to provide financial support to women with disabilities so that they may hire services to look after their children. Such support will be limited to two children for a period not exceeding two years.

IV. Children with Disabilities

32. Children with disabilities are the most vulnerable group and need special attention. The Government would strive to: -

    ➢ Ensure right to care, protection and security for children with disabilities;

    ➢ Ensure the right to development with dignity and equality creating an enabling environment where children can exercise their rights, enjoy equal opportunities and full participation in accordance with various statutes.

    ➢ Ensure inclusion and effective access to education, health, vocational training along with specialized rehabilitation services to children with disabilities.

    ➢ Ensure the right to development as well as recognition of special needs and of care, and protection of children with severe disabilities.

V. Barrier-free environment

33. Barrier-free environment enables people with disabilities to move about safely and freely, and use the facilities within the built environment. The goal of barrier free design is to provide an environment that supports the independent functioning of individuals so that they can participate without assistance, in every day activities. Therefore, to the maximum extent possible, buildings / places / transportation systems for public use will be made barrier free.

VI. Issue of Disability Certificates

34. The Government of India has notified guidelines for evaluation of the disabilities and procedure for certification. The Government will ensure that the persons with disabilities obtain the disability certificates without any difficulty in the shortest possible time by adoption of simple, transparent and client-friendly procedures.

VII. Social Security

35. Disabled persons, their families and care givers incur substantial additional expenditure for facilitating activities of daily living, medical care, transportation, assistive devices, etc. Therefore, there is a need to provide them social security by various means. Central Government has been providing tax relief to persons with disabilities and their guardians. The State Governments / U.T. Administrations have been providing unemployment allowance or disability pension. The State Governments will be encouraged to develop a comprehensive social security policy for persons with disabilities.

36. Parents of severely disabled persons with autism, cerebral palsy, mental retardation and multiple disabilities feel a sense of insecurity regarding the welfare of their wards after their death. National Trust for persons with autism, cerebral palsy, mental retardation and

multiple disabilities has been providing legal guardians through Local Level Committee. They are also implementing the Supported Guardianship Scheme to provide financial security to persons with the above-mentioned severe disabilities who are destitute and abandoned by supporting the cost of guardianship. This scheme, which is presently implemented in a few districts, shall be expanded to cover other areas in a phased manner.

VIII. Promotion of Non-Governmental Organizations (NGOs)

37. The National Policy recognizes the NGO sector as a very important institutional mechanism to provide affordable services to complement the endeavors of the Government. The NGO sector is a vibrant and growing one. It has played a significant role in the provisions of services for persons with disabilities. Some of the NGOs are also undertaking human resource development and research activities. Government has also been actively involving them in policy formulation, planning, implementation, monitoring and has been seeking their advice on various issues relating to persons with disabilities. Interaction with NGOs will be enhanced on various disability issues regarding planning, policy formulation and implementation. Networking, exchange of information and sharing of good practices amongst NGOs will be encouraged and facilitated. The following programmes will be undertaken:-

   ➤ A Directory of NGOs working in the field of disability will be prepared properly mapping them by geographic regions along with their major activities. For NGOs supported by the Central / State Governments, their resource position, both financial and manpower will also be reported. Disabled persons organizations, family associations and advocacy groups of parents of disabled persons shall also be covered in the directory identifying them separately.

> There are regional / State imbalances in the development of the NGO movement. Steps will be taken to encourage and accord preference to NGOs working in the underserved and inaccessible areas. Reputed NGOs shall also be encouraged to take up projects in such areas.

> NGOs will be encouraged to develop and adopt minimum standards, codes of conduct and ethics.

> NGOs will be provided opportunities for orientation and training of their human resource. Training in management skill which is already being provided, will be strengthened. Transparency, accountability, procedural simplification etc. will be guiding factors for improvement in the NGO-Government partnership.

> The NGOs shall be encouraged to mobilize their own resources to reduce the dependence on grants-in-aid from the Government and also to improve the availability of funds in the sector. Tapering of assistance in a schematic manner will also be considered so that the number of NGOs to be helped within the available resources could be maximized. Towards this end, NGOs will be trained in resource mobilization.

IX. Collection of regular information on Persons with Disabilities

38. There is a need for regular collection, compilation and analysis of data relating to socio-economic conditions of persons with disabilities. The National Sample Survey Organization has been collecting information on Socio-economic conditions of persons with disabilities on regular basis once in ten years since 1981. The Census has also started collection of information on persons with disabilities from the Census-2001. The National Sample Survey Organization will have to collect the information on persons with disabilities at least once in five years. The differences in the definitions adopted by the two agencies will be reconciled.

39. A comprehensive web site for persons with disability will be created under the Ministry of Social Justice & Empowerment. Organizations both in public and private sector will be encouraged to make their web sites accessible to the visually impaired using Screen Reading Technologies.

X. Research

40. For improving the quality of life of persons with disabilities, research will be supported on their socio-economic and cultural context, cause of disabilities, early childhood education methodologies, development of user-friendly aids and appliances and all matters connected with disabilities which will significantly alter the quality of their life and civil society's ability to respond to their concerns. Wherever persons with disabilities are subjected to research interventions, their or their family member or caregiver's consent is mandatory.

XI. Sports, Recreation and Cultural life

41. The contribution of sports for its therapeutic and community spirit is undeniable. Persons with disabilities have right to access sports, recreation and cultural facilities. The Government will take necessary steps to provide them opportunity for participation in various sports, recreation and cultural activities.

XII. Amendments to existing Acts dealing with the Persons with Disabilities

42. Twenty years have passed since the Persons with Disabilities (Equal Opportunities, Protection of Rights and Full Participation) Act, 1995 came into operation. With the experience gained in the implementation of the Act and developments in the disability sector, certain amendments to the Act have become necessary. These amendments will be carried out in consultation with the stakeholders. RCI and National Trust Acts will also be reviewed and if necessary, required amendments would be made.

Principal Areas of Intervention
I. Prevention, Early Detection and Intervention

43. In order to ensure prevention and early detection of disabilities, the following action will be taken:

   - National, regional and local programmes of immunization (for children as well as expectant mothers), public health and sanitation will be expanded.

   - Medical and para-medical personnel will be adequately trained and equipped for early detection of disability amongst children.

   - Training modules and facilities in disability prevention, early detection and intervention will be developed for medical and para medical health functionaries and Anganwadi workers.

   - Training programmes of postgraduate, undergraduate degree and diploma in medical education will include modules on disability prevention, early detection and interventions.

   - Disability specific manuals for families having persons with disabilities will also be developed and provided free of cost.

   - Human resource development institutions will ensure that the personnel needed to provide support services such as special education, clinical psychology, physiotherapy, occupational therapy, audiology, speech pathology, vocational counseling & training and social work are available in adequate numbers.

   - The latest research findings in the field of genetics will be utilized appropriately to minimize congenital disability including mental illness.

   - Appropriate plan of action for limiting effects of disability and prevention of secondary disabilities within the existing health delivery system will be evolved.

   - Attention will be paid towards improving awareness of nutrition, health care and sanitation amongst adolescent girls, expectant mothers and women in the reproductive period. Awareness programmes for prevention will be built in at the school level and at the level of teacher's training courses.

> Programmes will be undertaken for screening of children to identify at risk cases.

II. Programmes of Rehabilitation

44. Medical, educational and social rehabilitation programmes will be developed with the assistance of medical and rehabilitation professionals and with the participation of persons with disabilities and their families, legal guardians and communities. Convergence of Government programmes will be ensured and the following specific measures will be taken:

> State level centres for providing composite rehabilitation services including human resource development, research and long term specialized rehabilitation will be set up.

> Community based Rehabilitation programmes shall be encouraged. Self help groups of persons with disabilities and their family members/ caregivers shall be effectively involved in the process of rehabilitation.

> Setting up of mental health care homes for severely mental ill persons will be encouraged under district level Panchayati Raj institution with the involvement of NGOs. Alternatively, family support groups will be encouraged to setup Custodial Care Institutions for persons with mental disabilities without community and / or family support.

> Measures will also be taken to setup residential rehabilitation centres for providing vocational and social skills training for persons with mental disabilities.

III. Human Resource Development

45. The manpower will be developed in the following areas -

> Training of primary level workers both in health care and in community development comprising of Anganwadi workers, Auxiliary Nurses (Midwifes) etc.

➢ Support for training and orientation of personnel of Government and NGOs providing services.

➢ Training and sensitization of community decision makers such as members of Panchayats, head of families etc.

➢ Training and orientation of family members as caregivers.

46. Human resources will be trained to meet the requirement of education for children with disabilities under inclusive education, special education, home-based education, pre-school education etc, The following training programmes of different specialization and levels shall be developed:

➢ Training modules for teachers for inclusive education.

➢ Diploma, degree and high level programmes in special education

➢ Training of caregivers for home-based education and care services for disabled adults/ senior citizens etc.

47. Rehabilitation Council of India shall be the nodal agency for preparation of plans for training of rehabilitation personnel. The role of the National Institutes in disability specific training will be clearly spelt out and a five-year Plan of Action will be drawn up.

IV. Education of Persons with Disabilities

48. It will be ensured that every child with disability has access to appropriate pre-school, primary and secondary level education by 2020. Special care will be taken to -

➢ Make schools (building, approaches, toilets, playgrounds, laboratories, libraries etc.) barrier free and accessible for all types of disability.

➢ Medium and method of teaching will be suitably adapted to the requirements of most disability conditions.

➢ Technical / supplementary / specialized system of teaching / learning will be made available within the school or at a common center easily accessible to a cluster of schools.

➢ Teaching / learning tools and aids such as educational toys, Braille / talking books, appropriate software etc. will be made available. Incentives will be given to expand facilities for setting up of general libraries, e-libraries, Braille-libraries and talking books libraries, resource rooms etc.

➤ National Open School and distance learning programmes will be popularized and extended to other parts in the country.

➤ Sign language, Alternative and Augmentative Communications (AAC) and other modes as a viable medium in inter personal communication will be recognized, standardized and popularized.

➤ Schools will be located within easy traveling distance. Alternatively, viable travel arrangements will be made with the assistance of the community, State and NGOs.

➤ Parent-Teacher counseling and grievance redressal system will be set up in the schools.

➤ There will be separate mechanism to review annually the intake and retention of the girl child with disability at primary, secondary and higher levels of education.

➤ Many children with disabilities, who cannot join inclusive education system, would continue to get educational services from special schools. Special schools shall be appropriately re-modeled and re-oriented based on technological development. These schools will also help prepare children with disabilities to join mainstream inclusive education.

➤ In some cases due to the nature of disability (its type and degree), personal circumstances and preferences, home-based education will be provided.

➤ Course curriculum and evaluation system for children with various disabilities shall be developed keeping in view their capabilities. Examination system will be modified to make it disabled friendly by exemptions such as learning mathematics, learning only one language, etc. Further, facilities like extra time, use of calculators, use of Clarke's tables, scribes etc would be provided based on the requirement.

- Model Schools of Inclusive Education will be set up in each State / U.T to promote education of persons with disabilities.

- In the era of knowledge society, computers play very important role. Efforts will be made so that every child with disability gets suitably exposed to the use of computers.

- Children with disabilities upto the age of 6 years will be identified and necessary interventions made so that they are capable of joining inclusive education.

- Educational facilities will be provided in psychosocial rehabilitation centres for mentally ill persons.

- Many schools discourage enrollment of students on account of their disability due to lack of awareness about the capabilities of disabled persons. Programmes will be taken for sensitization of teachers, principals and other staff members in all schools.

- Special Schools presently being supported by the Ministry of Social Justice & Empowerment will incrementally become resource centres for inclusive education. Ministry of Human Resource Development shall open new special schools depending upon the requirement.

- Adult learning / leisure centers for adults with severe learning difficulties will be promoted.

- Three percent reservation for persons with disabilities in admission to higher educational institutions shall be enforced. Universities, colleges and professional institutions will be provided financial support to establish Disability Center to take care of educational needs of students with disabilities. They will also be encouraged to make classrooms, hostels, cafeterias and other facilities in the campus accessible to students with disabilities.

- Include a module in induction and in-service training programmes of teachers on issues relating to management of children with disabilities

49. The Ministry of Human Resource Development will be the nodal Ministry to coordinate all matters relating to the education of persons with disabilities.

V. Employment

50. The following steps will be taken for employment of persons with disabilities:

   - The government shall initiate a dialogue with private sector organizations to help persons with disabilities in getting employment.
   - Develop appropriate home-based income generation programmes for the persons with disabilities especially for persons with severe and multiple disabilities, who opt for such programmes. The system of coaching for employment will also be encouraged for persons with disabilities and their caregivers.
   - Facilitate modifications in the design of machinery, workstation and work environment necessary for the disabled persons to operate without barriers in training centres / factories / industry / offices etc.
   - Provide assistance through appropriate agencies like Marketing Boards, District Rural Development Agencies (DRDAs), private agencies and Non Governmental Organizations in marketing of goods and services produced by persons with disabilities.
   - Coverage of persons with disabilities in poverty alleviation programmes will be improved so that they get their due share of 3 percent as provided under statutory provisions.

VI. Barrier-free environment

51. For creation of barrier-free environment, the following strategies will be adopted:

   (i) Public buildings (functional or recreational), transport amenities including roads, sub-ways and pavements, railway platforms, bus-stops / terminals, ports, airports, modes of transports (bus, train, plane and waterways), playgrounds, open space etc. will be made accessible.

(ii) Use of sign language in all public functions will be encouraged.

(iii) Modification of Curriculum of Architects and Civil engineers will be undertaken to include issues relating to construction of barrier-free buildings. In service training will be provided on these issues to the government architects and engineers.

(v) Full adoption of comprehensive building byelaws and space standards for barrier-free built environment shall be ensured. Effort will be made to ensure adoption of the byelaws and space standards by all the states, municipal bodies and Panchayati Raj institutions in the country. These authorities will ensure that all newly constructed buildings for public use are barrier-free.

(vi) State Transport Undertakings will ensure disabled friendly features in their vehicles. Railways will provide barrier-free coaches in a phased manner. They will also make the platforms-buildings, toilets and other facilities barrier-free.

(vii) The Government will ensure that Industrial establishments, offices, public utilities both in public and private sector provide disabled friendly work place for their employees. Safety standards will be developed and strictly enforced.

(viii) Proactive steps will be taken to ensure disability-friendly IT environment in the country.

(ix) All the buildings, which are for public use, will be audited for its accessibility to persons with disability. There may be a need to develop professionally recognized access auditors whose services would be utilized for the purpose.

(x) Banking system will be encouraged to meet the needs to the persons with disabilities.

(xi) Communication needs of the persons with disabilities will be met by making information service and public documents accessible. Braille, tape-service, large print and other appropriate technologies will be used to provide information for the persons with visual disability.

VII. Social Protection

52. The following steps will be taken to provide adequate Social Security to the persons with disabilities:-

    ➤ A system of regular review of the policies of tax relief granted to the persons with disabilities will be put in place so that necessary income tax and other tax relief remain available to persons with disabilities.

    ➤ State Governments and UT Administrations will be encouraged to rationalize the amount of pension and unemployment allowance for persons with disabilities.

    ➤ Life Insurance Corporation of India has been providing insurance cover to persons with specific type of disabilities. There is a need to encourage all insurance agencies to cover persons with disabilities without exception.

VIII. Research

53. Research for developing new technologies for persons with disabilities will be encouraged with international cooperation, wherever necessary. Results of research will be widely disseminated. It will be focused on the following aspects:-

    ➤ Socio-cultural aspects of disability, which inter alia include study of social attitude and behavioral patterns towards persons with disabilities.

    ➤ Develop social indicators relating to the education of persons with disabilities so as to analyze the problems involved and take up programmes to improve access and opportunities

    ➤ Generate statistics about the employment status of persons by type of disability especially for those who become disabled due to accidents and other disasters.

    ➤ Study causes of different types and level of incidence of disabilities

    ➤ Genetic research to minimize incidence of disability under the aegis of Indian Council of Medical Research

> Adaptive technology research focusing on enhanced personal mobility, verbal / non-verbal communication, design changes in articles of every day usage etc. with a view to develop cost effective, user-friendly and durable aids & appliances with the help of premier technological institutes.

54. Ministry of Science & Technology shall set up Rehabilitation Technology Centre for coordinating and undertaking research and development, testing and certifying technologies, training etc. Appropriate hardware and software suitable for persons with disabilities to ensure access to information technologies will be developed.

IX. Sports, Recreation and Cultural activities

55. The following steps will be taken to ensure equal opportunities for sports, recreation and cultural activities: -

> Make places for recreation, cultural activities and sports, hotels, beaches, sports arenas, auditoriums, gym halls, etc. accessible.

> Travel agencies, hotels, voluntary organizations and others involved in organizing recreational activities or travel opportunities should offer their services to all, taking into account the special needs of persons with disabilities.

> Identification of talent amongst persons with disabilities in different sports shall be made with the assistance of local NGOs.

> Formation of Sports organizations and Cultural societies for persons with disabilities will be encouraged. There will be mechanism to support the participation of persons with disabilities in national and international events.

> A national award for excellence in sports for persons with disabilities shall be instituted.

RESPONSIBILITY FOR IMPLEMENTATION

56. The Ministry of Social Justice & Empowerment will be the nodal Ministry to coordinate all matters relating to the implementation of the Policy.

57. An inter-ministerial body to coordinate matters relating to implementation of National Policy will be formed. All stakeholders including prominent NGOs, Disabled Peoples Organizations, advocacy groups and family associations of parents / guardians, experts and professionals will also be represented on this body. Similar arrangements will be encouraged at the State and Districts levels. Panchayati Raj Institutions and Urban Local Bodies will be associated in the functioning of the District Disability Rehabilitation Centres' District Level Committees to coordinate the matters relating to the implementation of the policy.

58. The Ministries of Home Affairs, Health & Family Welfare, Rural Development, Urban Development, Youth Affairs & Sports, Railways, Science & Technology, Statistics & Programme Implementation, Labour, Panchayati Raj and Departments of Elementary Education & Literacy, Secondary & Higher Education, Road Transport & Highways, Public Enterprises, Revenue, Women & Child Development, Information Technology and Personnel & Training will setup necessary mechanism for implementation of the policy. A five-year perspective Plan and annual plans setting targets and financial allocations will be prepared by each Ministry / Department. The annual report of these Ministries / Departments will indicate progress achieved during the year.

59. The Chief Commissioner for Disabilities at Central level and State Commissioners at the State level shall play key role in implementation of National Policy, apart from their statutory responsibilities.

60. Panchayati Raj Institutions will play a crucial role in the implementation of the National Policy to address local level issues and draw up suitable programmes, which will be integrated with

the district and State plans. These institutions will include disability related components in their projects.

61. Infrastructure created during the course of implementation will be required to be maintained and effectively used for a long period. The community should take a leading role in generating resources with in themselves or through mobilization from private sector organizations to maintain the infrastructure and also to meet the running cost. This step will not only reduce the burden on state resources but will also create a greater sense of responsibility among the community and private entrepreneurs.

62. Every five years a comprehensive review will be done on the implementation of the National Policy. A document indicating status of implementation and a roadmap for five years shall be prepared based on the deliberations in a national level convention. State Governments and Union Territory administrations will be urged to take steps for drawing up State Policy and develop action plan.

CONSOLIDATED INSTRUCTIONS OF DOP&T ON 3%
RESERVATION
No.336035/3/2004-Estt (Res)
GOVERNMENT OF INDIA
MINISTRY OF PERSONNEL, PUBLIC GRIEVANCES &
PENSIONS
DEPARTMENT OF PERSONNEL & TRAINING
****

New Delhi, Dated the 29th December, 2005
OFFICE MEMORANDUM
Subject: Reservation for the Persons with Disabilities

———-

With a view to consolidating the existing instructions, bringing them in line with the Persons with Disabilities (Equal Opportunities, Protection of Rights & Full Participation) Act, 1995 and clarifying certain issues including procedural matters, the following instructions are issued with regard to reservation for persons with disabilities (physically handicapped persons) in posts and services under the Government of India. These instructions shall supercede all previous instructions issued on the subject so far.

2. QUANTUM OF RESERVATION: Three percent of the vacancies in case of direct recruitment to Group A, B, C & D posts shall be reserved for persons with disabilities of which one per cent each shall be reserved for persons suffering from (i) blindness or low vision, (ii) hearing impairment and (iii) locomotor disability or cerebral palsy in the posts identified for each disability;

Three percent of the vacancies in case of promotion to Group D, and Group C posts in which the element of direct recruitment, if any, does not exceed 75%, shall be reserved for persons with disabilities of which one per cent each shall be reserved for persons suffering from (i) blindness or low vision, (ii) hearing impairment and (iii) locomotor disability or cerebral palsy in the posts identified for each disability.

3. EXEMPTION FROM RESERVATION: If any Department/Ministry considers it necessary to exempt any establishment partly or fully from the provision of reservation for persons with disabilities, it may make a reference to the Ministry of Social Justice and Employment giving full justification for the proposal. The grant of exemption shall be consider by an Inter-Departmental Committee set up by the Ministry of Social Justice and Empowerment.

4. IDENTIFICATION OF JOBS/POSTS: The Ministry of Social Justice and Empowerment have identified the jobs/posts suitable to be held by persons with disabilities and the physically requirement for all such jobs/posts vide their notification no. 16-25/99. NI.I dated 3.5.2001. The jobs/posts given in Annexure II of the said notification as amended from time to time shall be used to give effect to 3 per cent reservation to the persons with disabilities. It may, however, be noted that:

    ➢ The nomenclature used for any job/post shall mean and include nomenclature used for other comparable jobs/posts having identical functions.

    ➢ The list of jobs/posts notified by the Ministry of Social Justice & Empowerment is not exhaustive. The concerned Ministries/ Departments shall have the discretion to identify jobs/posts in addition to the jobs/posts already identified by the Ministry of Social Justice & Empowerment. However, no Ministry/ Department/Establishment shall exclude any identified job/ post from the purview of reservation at its own discretion.

    ➢ If a job/post identified for persons with disabilities is shifted from one group or grade to another group or grade due to change in the pay-scale or otherwise, the job/post shall remain identified.

5. RESERVATION IN POSTS IDENTIFIED FOR ONE OR TWO CATEGORIES: If a post is identified suitable only for one category of disability, reservation in that post shall be given to persons with that disability only. Reservation of 3% shall not be reduced in such cases and total reservation in the post will be given to persons

suffering from the disability for which it has been identified. Likewise in case the post is identified suitable for two categories of disabilities, reservation shall be distributed between persons with those categories of disabilities equally, as far as possible. It shall, however, be ensured that reservation in different posts in the establishment is distributed in such a way that the persons of three categories of disabilities, as far as possible, get equal representation.

6. APPOINTMENT AGAINST UNRESERVED VACANCIES: In the posts which are identified suitable for persons with disabilities, a person with disability cannot be denied the right to compete for appointment against an unreserved vacancy. Thus a person with disability can be appointed against an unreserved vacancy, provided the post is identified suitable for persons with disability of the relevant category.

7. ADJUSTMENT OF CANDIDATES SELECTED ON THEIR OWN MERIT: Persons with disabilities selected on their own merit without relaxed standards alongwith other candidates, will not be adjusted against the reserved share of vacancies. The reserved vacancies will be filled up separately from amongst the eligible candidates with disabilities which will thus comprise physically handicapped candidates who are lower in merit than the last candidate in merit list but otherwise found suitable for appointment, if necessary, by relaxed standards. It wjll apply in case of direct recruitment as well as promotion, wherever reservation for persons with disabilities is admissible.

8. DEFINITIONS OF DISABILITIES: Definitions of categories of disabilities for the purpose of this Office Memorandum are given below:

(i) (a) Blindness: "Blindness" refers to a condition where a person suffers from any of the following conditions, namely:-

> total absence of sight; or

> visual acuity not exceeding 6/60 or 20/200(snellen) in the better eye with correcting lenses; or

> limitation of the field of vision subtending an angle of 20 degree or worse;

(b) Low vision: "Person with low vision" means a person with impairment of visual functioning even after treatment or standard refractive correction but who uses or is potentially capable of using vision for the planning or execution of a task with appropriate assistive device.

(ii) Hearing Impairment: "Hearing Impairment" means loss of sixty decibels or more in the better ear in the conversational range of frequencies.

(iii) (a) Locomotor disability: "Locomotor disability" means disability of the bones, joints or muscles leading to substantial restriction of the movement of the limbs or any form of cerebral palsy.

(b) Cerebral Palsy: "Cerebral Palsy" means a group of non-progressive conditions of a person characterised by abnormal motor control posture resulting from brain insult or injuries occurring in the pre-natal, peri-natal or infant period of development.

(c) All the cases of orthopaedically handicapped persons would be covered under the category of "locomotor disability or cerebral palsy."

9. DEGREE OF DISABILITY FOR RESERVATION: Only such persons would be eligible for reservation in services / posts who suffer from not less than 40 per cent of relevant disability. A person who wants to avail of benefit of reservation would have to submit a Disability Certificate issued by a competent authority in the format given in Annexure I.

10. COMPETENT AUTHORITY TO ISSUE DISABILITY CERTIFICATE: The competent authority to issue Disability Certificate shall be a Medical Board duly constituted by the Central or a State Government. The Central/State Government may constitute Medical Board(s) consisting of at least three members out of which at least one shall be a specialist in the particular field tor assessing locomotor / cerebral/visual / hearing disability, as the case may be.

11. The Medical Board shall, after due examination, give a permanent disability certificate in cases of such permanent disabilities where there are no chances of variation in the degree of disability. The Medical Board shall indicate the period of validity of the certificate, in cases where there are chances of variation in the degree of disability. No refusal of disability certificate shall be made unless an opportunity is given to the applicant of being heard. On representation by the applicant, the Medical Board may review its decision having regard to all the facts and circumstances of the case and pass such orders in the matter as it thinks fit..

12. At the time of initial appointment and promotion against a vacancy reserved for persons with disability, the appointing authority shall ensure that the candidate is eligible to get the benefit of reservation..

13. COMPUTATION OF RESERVATION: Reservation for persons with disabilities in case of Group C and Group D posts shall be computed on the basis of total number of vacancies occurring in all Group C or Group D posts, as the case may be, in the establishment, although the recruitment of the persons with disabilities would only be in the posts identified suitable for them. The number of vacancies to be reserved for the persons with disabilities in case of direct recruitment to Group 'C' posts in an establishment shall be computed by taking into account the total number of vacancies arising in Group 'C' posts for being filled by direct recruitment in a recruitment year both in the identified and non-identified posts under the establishment. The same procedure shall apply for Group 'D' posts. Similarly, all vacancies in promotion quota shall be taken into account while computing reservation in promotion in Group 'C' and Group 'D' posts. Since reservation is limited to identified posts only and number of vacancies reserved is computed on the basis of total vacancies (in identified posts as well as unidentified posts), it is possible that number of

14. Reservaton for persons with disabilities in Group' A ' posts shall be computed on the basis of vacancies occurring in direct recruitment quota in all the identified Group' A ' posts in the establishment. The same method of computation applies for Group 'B' posts.

15. EFFECTING RESERVATION -MAINTENANCE OF ROSTERS:

> All establishments shall maintain separate 100 point reservation roster registers in the format given in Annexure II for determining / effecting reservation for the disabled -one each for Group' A ' posts filled by direct recruitment, Group 'B' posts filled by direct recruitment, Group 'C' posts filled by direct recruitment, Group 'C' posts filled by promotion, Group 'D' posts filled by direct recruitment and Group' D ' posts filled by promotion.

> Each register shall have cycles of 100 points and each cycle of l00 points shall be divided into three blocks, comprising the following points:
> - 1st Block -point No.1 to point No.33
> - 2nd Block -point No.34 to point No.66
> - 3rd Block -point No.67 to point No.100

> Points I, 34 and 67 of the roster shall be earmarked reserved for persons with disabilities -one point for each of the three categories of disabilities. The head of the establishment shall decide the categories of disabilities for which the points I, 34 and 67 will be reserved keeping in view all relevant facts.

> All the vacancies in Group C posts falling in direct recruitment quota arising in the establishment shall be entered in the relevant roster register. If the post falling at point no.1 is not identified for the disabled or the head of the establishment considers it desirable not to fill it up by a disabled person or it is not possible to fill up that post by the disabled for any other reason, one of the vacancies falling at any of the points from 2 to 33 shall be treated as reserved for the disabled and filled as such. Likewise a vacancy falling at any of the points from 34 to 66 or from 67 to 100 shall

be filled by the disabled. The purpose of keeping points I, 34 and 67 as reserved is to fill up the first available suitable vacancy from 1 to 33, first available suitable vacancy from 34 to 66 and first available suitable vacancy from 67 to 100 by persons with disabilities.

➤ There is a possibility that none of the vacancies from 1 to 33 is suitable for any category of the disabled. In that case two vacancies from 34 to 66 shall be filled as reserved for persons with disabilities. If the vacancies from 34 to 66 are also not suitable for any category, three vacancies shall be filled as reserved from the third block containing points from 67 to 100. This means that if no vacancy can be reserved in a particular block, it shall be carried into the next block.

➤ After all the 100 points of the roster are covered, a fresh cycle of 100 points shall start.

➤ If the number of vacancies in a year is such as to cover only one block or two, discretion as to which category' of the disabled should be accommodated first shall vest in the head of the establishment, who shall decide on the basis of the nature of the post, the level of representation of the specific disabled category in the concerned grade/post etc.

➤ A separate roster shall be maintained for group C posts filled by promotion and procedure as explained above shall be followed for giving reservation to persons with disabilities. Likewise two separate rosters shall be maintained for Group D posts, one for the posts filled by direct recruitment and another for posts filled by promotion.

➤ Reservation in group A and group B posts is determined on the basis of vacancies in the identified posts only. Separate rosters for Group A posts and Group B posts in the establishment shall be maintained. In the rosters maintained for Group A and Group B posts, all vacancies of direct recruitment arising in identified posts shall be entered and reservation shall be effected the same way as explained above.

16. **INTER SE EXCHANGE AND CARRY FORWARD OF RESERVATION IN CASE OF DIRECT RECRUITMENT:**

  ➢ Reservation for each of the three categories of persons with disabilities shall be made separately. But if the nature of vacancies in an establishment is such that a person of a specific category of disability cannot be employed, the vacancies may be interchanged among the three categories with the approval of the Ministry of Social Justice & Empowerment and reservation may be determined and vacancies filled accordingly.

  ➢ If any vacancy reserved for any category of disability cannot be filled due to non-availability of a suitable person with that disability or, for any other sufficient reason, such vacancy shall not be filled and shall be carried forward as a 'backlog reserved vacancy' to the subsequent recruitment year.

  ➢ In the subsequent recruitment year the 'backlog reserved vacancy' shall be treated as reserved for the category of disability for which it was kept reserved in the initial year of recruitment. However, if a suitable person with that disability is not available, it may be filled by interchange among the three categories of disabilities. In case no suitable person with disability is available for filling up the post in the subsequent year also, the employer may fill up the vacancy by appointment of a person other than a person with disability. If the vacancy is filled by a person with disability of the category for which it was reserved or by a person of other category of disability by inter se exchange in the subsequent recruitment year, it will be treated to have been filled by reservation. But if the vacancy is filled by a person other than a person with disability in the subsequent recruitment year, reservation shall be carried forward for a further period upto two recruitment years whereafter the reservation shall lapse. In these two subsequent years, if situation so arises, the procedure for filling up the reserved vacancy shall be the same as followed in the first subsequent recruitment year.

17. In order to ensure that cases of. lapse of reservation are kept to the minimum, any recruitment of the disabled candidates shall first be counted against the additional quota brought forward from previous years, if any, in their chronological order. If candidates are not available for all the vacancies, the older carried forward reservation would be filled first and the relatively later carried forward reservation would be further carried forward.

18. CONSIDERATION ZONE. INTERSE EXCHANGE AND FORWARD OF RESERVATION IN CASE OF PROMOTION

   ➤ While filling up the reserved vacancies by promotion by selection, the disabled candidates who are within the normal zone of consideration shall be considered for promotion. Where adequate number of disabled candidates of the appropriate category of handicap are not available within the normal zone, the zone of consideration may be extended to five times the number of vacancies and the persons with disabilities falling within the extended zone may be considered. In the event of non availability of candidates even in the extended zone, the reservation can be exchanged so that post can be filled by a person with other category of disability, if possible. If it is not possible to fill up the post by reservation, the post may be filled by a person other than a person with disability and the reservation shall be carried forward for upto three subsequent recruitment years, whereafter it shall lapse.

   ➤ In posts filled by promotion by non-selection, the eligible candidates with disabilities shall be considered for promotion against the reserved vacancies and in case no eligible candidate of the appropriate category of disability is available, the vacancy can be exchanged with other categories of disabilities identified for it. If it is not possible to fill up the post by reservation even by exchange, the reservation shall be carried forward for upto three subsequent recruitment years whereafter it shall lapse.

19. HORIZONTALITY OF RESERVATION FOR PERSONS WITH DISABILITIES: Reservation for backward classes of citizens (SCs, STs and OBCs) is called vertical reservation and the reservation for categories such as persons with disabilities and ex-servicemen is called horizontal reservation. Horizontal reservation cuts across vertical reservation (in what is called inter-locking reservation) and persons selected against the quota for persons with disabilities have to be placed. in the appropriate category viz.SC/ST/OBC/General candidates depending upon the category to which they belong in the roster meant for reservation of SCs/STs/OBCs. To illustrate, if in a given year there are two vacancies reserved for the persons with disabilities and out of two persons with disabilities appointed, one belongs to a Scheduled Caste and the other to general category then the disabled SC candidate shall be adjusted against the SC point in the reservation roster and the general candidate against unreserved point in the relevant reservation roster. In case none of the vacancies falls on point reserved for the SCs, the disabled candidate belonging to SC shall be adjusted in future against the next available vacancy reserved for SCs.

20. Since the persons with disabilities have to be placed in the appropriate category viz. SC/ST/OBC/ General in the roster meant for reservation of SCs/STs/OBCs, the application form for the post should require the candidates applying under the quota reserved for persons with disabilities to indicate whether they belong to SC/ST/OBC or General category.

21. RELAXATION IN AGE LIMIT: Upper age limit for persons with disabilities shall be relaxable (a) by ten years (15 years for SCs/STs and 13 years for OBCs) in case of direct recruitment to Group 'C' and Group 'D' posts; (b) by 5 years (10 years for SCs/STs and 8 years for OBCs) in case of direct recruitment to Group' A' and Group 'B' posts where recruitment is made otherwise than through open competitive examination; and (c) by 10 years (15 years for SCs/STs and 13 years for OBCs) in case of direct recruitment to Group A and Group B posts through open competitive examination.

Relaxation in age limit shall be applicable irrespective of the fact whether the post is reserved or not, provided the post is identified suitable for persons with disabilities.

22. RELAXATION OF STANDARD OF SUITABILITY: If sufficient number of persons with disabilities are not available on the basis of the general standard to fill all the vacancies reserved for them, candidates belonging to this category may be selected 0:!1 relaxed standard to fill up the remaining vacancies reserved for them provided they are not found unfit for such post or posts. Thus, to the extent the number of vacancies reserved for persons with disabilities cannot be filled on the basis of general standards, candidates belonging to this category may be taken by relaxing the standards to make up the deficiency in the reserved quota subject to the fitness of these candidates for appointment to the post / posts in question.

23. MEDICAL EXAMINATION: As per Rule 10 of the Fundamental Rules, every new entrant to Government Service on initial appointment is required to produce a medical certificate of fitness issued by a competent authority. In case of medical examination of a person with disability for appointment to a post identified as suitable to be held by a person suffering from a particular kind of disability, the concerned Medical Officer or Board shall be informed beforehand that the post is identified suitable to be held by persons with disability of the relevant category and the candidate shall then be examined medically keeping this fact in view.

24. EXEMPTION FROM PAYMENT OF EXAMINATION FEE AND APPLICATION FEE: Persons with disabilities shall be exempt from payment of application fee and examination fee, prescribed in respect of competitive examinations held by the Staff Selection Commission, the Union Public Service Commission etc. for recruitment to various posts. This exemption shall be available only to such persons who would otherwise be eligible for appointment to the post on the basis of standards of medical fitness prescribed for that post (including any concession specifically extended to

the disabled persons) and who enclose with the application form, necessary certificate from a competent authority in support of their claim of disability.

25. NOTICE OF VACANCIES: In order to ensure that persons with disabilities get a fair opportunity in consideration for appointment to an identified post, the following points shall be kept in view while sending the requisition notice to the Employment Exchange, the SSC, the UPSC etc. and while advertising the vacancies:-

> Number of vacancies reserved for SCs/STs/OBCs/Ex-Servicemen/Persons suffering from Blindness or Low Vision/ Persons suffering from Hearing ImpainnentlPersons suffering from Locomotor Disability or Cerebral Palsy should be indicated clearly.

> In case of vacancies in posts identified suitable to be held by persons with disability. it shall be indicated that the post is identified for persons with disabilities suffering from blindness or low vision; hearing impairment; and/or locomotor disability or cerebral palsy, as the case may be, and that the persons with disabilities belonging to the category/categories for which the post is identified shall be allowed to apply even if no vacancies are reserved for them. Such candidates will be considered for selection for appointment to the post by general standards of merit.

> In case of vacancies in posts identified suitable for persons with disabilities, irrespective of whether any vacancies are reserved or not, the categories of disabilities viz blindness or low vision, hearing impairment and locomotor disability or cerebral palsy, for which the post is identified suitable alongwith functional classification and physical requirements for performing the duties attached to the post shall be indicated clearly.

> It shall also be indicated that persons suffering from not less than 40% of the relevant disability shall alone be eligible for the benefit of reservation.

26. CERTIFICATE BY REQUISITIONING AUTHORITY: In order to ensure proper implementation of the provisions of reservation for persons with disabilities, the requisitioning authority while sending the requisition to the UPSC, SSC etc. for filling up of posts shall furnish the following certificate to the recruiting agency:-

"It is certified that the requirements of the Persons with Disabilities (Equal Opportunities, Protection of Rights & Full Participation) Act, 1995 and the policy relating to reservation for persons with disabilities has been taken care of while sending this requisition. The vacancies reported in this requisition fall at points no. of cycle no. of 100 point reservation roster out of which. number of vacancies are reserved for persons with disabilities."

27. ANNUAL REPORTS REGARDING REPRESENTATION OF PERSONS WIH DISABILITIES:

    (i) Soon after the first of January of every year, each appointing authority shall send to its administrative Ministry/Department:-

    PWD Report-I in the prescribed proforma (Annexure III) showing the total number of employees, total number of employees in the posts which have been identified suitable for persons with disabilities and number of employees suffering from blindness or low vision, hearing impairment, and locomotor disability or cerebral palsy as on the 1 st January of the year, and PWD Report-II in the prescribed proforma (Annexure IV) showing the number of vacancies reserved for persons suffering from blindness or low vision, hearing impairment, and locomotor disability or cerebral palsy and number of such persons actually appointed during the preceding calendar year.

    (ii) The administrative Ministry/Department shall scrutinize the information received from all appointing authorities under it and send consolidated PWD Report-I and PWD Report- II in prescribed performa in respect of the Ministry/Department including information in respect of all attached and subordinate offices under its control to the Department of Personnel and Training by the 31st March of each year.

(iii) The following points may be kept in view while sending the reports to the Department of Personnel & Training:-

The reports sent to the DOPT should not include information in respect of public sector undertakings, statutory, semi-Government and autonomous bodies. Statutory, semi-Government and autonomous bodies shall furnish consolidated information in the prescribed proforma to the administrative Ministry/Department concerned who may scrutinize, monitor and maintain it at their own level. The Department of Public Enterprises may collect similar information in respect of all public sector undertakings.

The attached/subordinate offices shall send information to their administrative Ministry/Department only and shall not send it direct to this Department.

The figures in respect of persons with disabilities shall include persons appointed by reservation as well as appointed otherwise.

The PWD Report I relates to persons and not to posts. Therefore, while furnishing this report the posts vacant etc. should not be taken into account. In this report persons on deputation should be included in the establishment of the borrowing Ministry/Department/Office and not in the parent establishment. Persons permanent in one grade but officiating or holding temporary appointment in the higher grade shall be included in the figures relating to the Class of service to which the higher grade belongs.

28. LIAISON OFFICER FOR PERSONS WITH DISABILITIES: Liaison Officers appointed to look after reservation matters for SCs/STs shall also work as Liaison Officers for reservation matters relating to persons with disabilities and shall ensure compliance of these instructions.

29. All the Ministries/Departments are requested to bring the above instructions to the notice of all appointing authorities under their control.

India's Disability Act of 1995 provides various facilities for both children and adults with disabilities in India. Under the Disabilities Act of India, children with disabilities have the right to free education until they reach the age of eighteen in schools that are integrated, or in 'special,' schools. Children with disabilities have the right to appropriate transportation, removal of architectural barriers, as well as the restructuring of curriculum and modifications in the examination system. Scholarships, uniforms, books, and teaching materials are all provided to children with disabilities for free in India.

The nation of India currently has four different laws that pertain to people with disabilities. These laws are:

➤ The Mental Health Act1987, The Persons with disabilities Act, The Rehabilitation Council of India act, The National Trust for welfare of Persons with Austism, Cerebral Palsy, Mental Retardation and Multiple Disabilities Act 1999

The Rights of Persons with Disabilities Act, 2016

ARRANGEMENT OF SECTIONS

CHAPTER I PRELIMINARY

SECTIONS

Short title and commencement.

Definitions.

CHAPTER II RIGHTS AND ENTITLEMENTS

Equality and non-discrimination.

Women and children with disabilities.

Community life.

Protection from cruelty and inhuman treatment.

Protection from abuse, violence and exploitation.

Protection and safety.

Home and family.

Reproductive rights.

Accessibility in voting.

Access to justice.

Legal capacity.

Provision for guardianship.

Designation of authorities to support.

1.   Duty of educational institutions.

CHAPTER III EDUCATION

Specific measures to promote and facilitate inclusive education.

Adult education.

CHAPTER IV

SKILL DEVELOPMENT AND EMPLOYMENT

Vocational training and self-employment.

Non-discrimination in employment.

Equal opportunity policy.

Maintenance of records.

Appointment of Grievance Redressal Officer.

CHAPTER V

SOCIAL SECURITY, HEALTH, REHABILITATION AND RECREATION

Social security.

Healthcare.

Insurance schemes.

SECTIONS

Rehabilitation.

Research and development.

Culture and recreation.

Sporting activities.

CHAPTER VI

SPECIAL PROVISIONS FOR PERSONS WITH BENCHMARK DISABILITIES

Free education for children with benchmark disabilities.

Reservation in higher educational institutions.

Identification of posts for reservation.

Reservation.

Incentives to employers in private sector.

Special employment exchange.

Special schemes and development programmes.

CHAPTER VII
SPECIAL PROVISIONS FOR PERSONS WITH DISABILITIES WITH HIGH SUPPORT NEEDS

Special provisions for persons with disabilities with high support.

CHAPTER VIII
DUTIES AND RESPONSIBILITIES OF APPROPRIATE GOVERNMENTS

Awareness campaigns.

Accessibility.

Access to transport.

Access to information and communication technology.

Consumer goods.

Mandatory observance of accessibility norms.

Time limit for making existing infrastructure and premises accessible and action for that purpose.

Time limit for accessibility by service providers.

Human resource development.

Social audit.

CHAPTER IX
REGISTRATION OF INSTITUTIONS FOR PERSONS WITH DISABILITIES AND GRANTS TO SUCH INSTITUTIONS

Competent authority.

Registration.

Application and grant of certificate of registration.

Revocation of registration.

Appeal.

Act not to apply to institutions established or maintained by Central or State Government.

Assistance to registered institutions.

CHAPTER X CERTIFICATION OF SPECIFIED DISABILITIES

Guidelines for assessment of specified disabilities.

SECTIONS

Designation of certifying authorities.

Procedure for certification.

Appeal against a decision of certifying authority.

CHAPTER XI

CENTRAL AND STATE ADVISORY BOARDS ON DISABILITY AND DISTRICT LEVEL COMMITTEE

Constitution of Central Advisory Board on Disability.

Terms and conditions of service of members.

Disqualifications.

Vacation of seats by Members.

Meetings of the Central Advisory Board on disability.

Functions of Central Advisory Board on disability.

State Advisory Board on disability.

Terms and conditions of service of Members.

Disqualification.

Vacation of seats.

Meetings of State Advisory Board on disability.

Functions of State Advisory Board on disability.

District-level Committee on disability.

Vacancies not to invalidate proceedings.

CHAPTER XII

CHIEF COMMISSIONER AND STATE COMMISSIONER FOR PERSONS WITH DISABILITIES

Appointment of Chief Commissioner and Commissioners.

Functions of Chief Commissioner.

Action of appropriate authorities on recommendation of Chief Commissioner.

CHAPTER XIII SPECIAL COURT

CHAPTER XIV

NATIONAL FUND FOR PERSONS WITH DISABILITIES

CHAPTER XV

STATE FUND FOR PERSONS WITH DISABILITIES

CHAPTER XVI OFFENCES AND PENALTIES

Previous sanction of appropriate Government.

Alternative punishments.

CHAPTER XVII MISCELLANEOUS

Application of other laws not barred.

Protection of action taken in good faith.

Power to remove difficulties.

Power to amend Schedule.

Power of Central Government to make rules.

Power of State Government to make rules.

Repeal and savings. THE SCHEDULE.

THE RIGHTS OF PERSONS WITH DISABILITIES ACT, 2016
ACT NO. 49 OF 2016

[*27th December, 2016*]

An Act to give effect to the United Nations Convention on the Rights of Persons with Disabilities and for matters connected therewith or incidental thereto.

WHEREAS the United Nations General Assembly adopted its Convention on the Rights of Persons with Disabilities on the 13th day of December, 2006.

AND WHEREAS the aforesaid Convention lays down the following principles for empowerment of persons with disabilities,—

(a) respect for inherent dignity, individual autonomy including the freedom to make one's own choices, and independence of persons;

(b) non-discrimination;

(c) full and effective participation and inclusion in society;

(d) respect for difference and acceptance of persons with disabilities as part of human diversity and humanity;

(e) equality of opportunity;

(f) accessibility;

(g) equality between men and women;

(h) respect for the evolving capacities of children with disabilities and respect for the right of children with disabilities to preserve their identities;

AND WHEREAS India is a signatory to the said Convention;

AND WHEREAS India ratified the said Convention on the 1st day of October, 2007; AND WHEREAS it is considered necessary to implement the Convention aforesaid.

BE it enacted by Parliament in the Sixty-seventh Year of the Republic of India as follows:—

CHAPTER I: PRELIMINARY

1. Short title and commencement.[1]—

(1) This Act may be called the Rights of Persons with Disabilities Act, 2016.

(2) It shall come into force on such [1]date as the Central Government may, by notification in the Official Gazette, appoint.

2. Definitions.—In this Act, unless the context otherwise requires,—

(a) "appellate authority" means an authority notified under sub-section (3) of section 14 or sub-section (1) of section 53 or designated under sub-section (1) of section 59, as the case may be;

(b) "appropriate Government" means,—

  (i) in relation to the Central Government or any establishment wholly or substantially financed by that Government, or a Cantonment Board constituted under the Cantonments Act, 2006 (41 of 2006), the Central Government;

  (ii) in relation to a State Government or any establishment, wholly or substantially financed by that Government, or any local authority, other than a Cantonment Board, the State Government.

(c) "barrier" means any factor including communicational, cultural, economic, environmental, institutional, political, social, attitudinal or structural factors which hampers the full and effective participation of persons with disabilities in society;

(d) "care-giver" means any person including parents and other family Members who with or without payment provides care, support or assistance to a person with disability;

(e) "certifying authority" means an authority designated under sub-section (1) of section 57;

(f) "communication" includes means and formats of communication, languages, display of text, Braille, tactile communication, signs, large print, accessible multimedia, written, audio, video, visual displays,

---

[1] 19th April, 2017, *vide* notification no. S.O. 1215 (E) dated 19th April, 2017, *see* Gazette of India, Extraordinary, Part II, Section 3 (ii).

sign language, plain-language, human-reader, augmentative and alternative modes and accessible information and communication technology;

(g) "competent authority" means an authority appointed under section 49;

(h) "discrimination" in relation to disability, means any distinction, exclusion, restriction on the basis of disability which is the purpose or effect of impairing or nullifying the recognition, enjoyment or exercise on an equal basis with others of all human rights and fundamental freedoms in the political, economic, social, cultural, civil or any other field and includes all forms of discrimination and denial of reasonable accommodation;

(i) "establishment" includes a Government establishment and private establishment;

(j) "Fund" means the National Fund constituted under section 86;

(k) "Government establishment" means a corporation established by or under a Central Act or State Act or an authority or a body owned or controlled or aided by the Government or a local authority or a Government company as defined in section 2 of the Companies Act, 2013 (18 of 2013) and includes a Department of the Government;

(l) "high support" means an intensive support, physical, psychological and otherwise, which may be required by a person with benchmark disability for daily activities, to take independent and informed decision to access facilities and participating in all areas of life including education, employment, family and community life and treatment and therapy;

(m) "inclusive education" means a system of education wherein students with and without disability learn together and the system of teaching and learning is suitably adapted to meet the learning needs of different types of students with disabilities;

(n) "information and communication technology" includes all services and innovations relating to information and communication, including telecom services, web based services, electronic and print services, digital and virtual services;

(o) "institution" means an institution for the reception, care, protection, education, training, rehabilitation and any other activities for persons with disabilities;

(p) "local authority" means a Municipality or a Panchayat, as defined in clause (*e*) and clause (*f*) of article 243P of the Constitution; a Cantonment Board constituted under the Cantonments Act, 2006 (41 of 2006); and any other authority established under an Act of Parliament or a State Legislature to administer the civic affairs;

(q) "notification" means a notification published in the Official Gazette and the expression "notify" or "notified" shall be construed accordingly;

(r) "person with benchmark disability" means a person with not less than forty per cent. of a specified disability where specified disability has not been defined in measurable terms and includes a person with disability where specified disability has been defined in measurable terms, as certified by the certifying authority;

(s) "person with disability" means a person with long term physical, mental, intellectual or sensory impairment which, in interaction with barriers, hinders his full and effective participation in society equally with others;

(t) "person with disability having high support needs" means a person with benchmark disability certified under clause (*a*) of sub-section (*2*) of section 58 who needs high support;

(u) "prescribed" means prescribed by rules made under this Act;

(v) "private establishment" means a company, firm, cooperative or other society, associations, trust, agency, institution, organisation, union, factory or such other establishment as the appropriate Government may, by notification, specify;

(w) "public building" means a Government or private building, used or accessed by the public at large, including a building used for educational or vocational purposes, workplace, commercial activities, public utilities, religious, cultural, leisure or recreational activities, medical or health services, law enforcement agencies, reformatories or judicial foras, railway stations or platforms, roadways bus stands or terminus, airports or waterways;

(x) "public facilities and services" includes all forms of delivery of services to the public at large, including housing, educational and vocational trainings, employment and career advancement, shopping or marketing, religious, cultural, leisure or recreational, medical, health and rehabilitation, banking, finance and insurance, communication, postal and information, access to justice, public utilities, transportation;

(y) "reasonable accommodation" means necessary and appropriate modification and adjustments, without imposing a disproportionate or undue burden in a particular case, to ensure to persons with disabilities the enjoyment or exercise of rights equally with others;

(z) "registered organisation" means an association of persons with disabilities or a disabled person organisation, association of parents of persons with disabilities, association of persons with disabilities and family members, or a voluntary or non-governmental or charitable organisation or trust, society, or non-profit company working for the welfare of the persons with disabilities, duly registered under an Act of Parliament or a State Legislature;

(*za*) "rehabilitation" refers to a process aimed at enabling persons with disabilities to attain and maintain optimal, physical, sensory, intellectual, psychological environmental or social function levels;

(*zb*) "Special Employment Exchange" means any office or place established and maintained by the Government for the collection and furnishing of information, either by keeping of registers or otherwise, regarding—

(i) persons who seek to engage employees from amongst the persons with disabilities;

(ii) persons with benchmark disability who seek employment;

(iii) vacancies to which persons with benchmark disabilities seeking employment may be appointed;

(*zc*) "specified disability" means the disabilities as specified in the Schedule;

(*zd*) "transportation systems" includes road transport, rail transport, air transport, water transport, para transit systems for the last mile connectivity, road and street infrastructure, etc;

(*ze*) "universal design" means the design of products, environments, programmes and services to be usable by all people to the greatest extent possible, without the need for adaptation or specialised design and shall apply to assistive devices including advanced technologies for particular group of persons with disabilities.

CHAPTER II: RIGHTS AND ENTITLEMENTS

1.   Equality and non-discrimination.

(1)   The appropriate Government shall ensure that the persons with disabilities enjoy the right to equality, life with dignity and respect for his or her integrity equally with others.

(2)   The appropriate Government shall take steps to utilise the capacity of persons with disabilities by providing appropriate environment.

(3)   No person with disability shall be discriminated on the ground of disability, unless it is shown that the impugned act or omission is a proportionate means of achieving a legitimate aim.

(4)   No person shall be deprived of his or her personal liberty only on the ground of disability.

(5)   The appropriate Government shall take necessary steps to ensure reasonable accommodation for persons with disabilities.

2.   Women and children with disabilities.

(1)   The appropriate Government and the local authorities shall take measures to ensure that the women and children with disabilities enjoy their rights equally with others.

(2)   The appropriate Government and local authorities shall ensure that all children with disabilities shall have right on an equal basis to freely express their views on all matters affecting them and provide them appropriate support keeping in view their age and disability.".

3. Community life.

(1) The persons with disabilities shall have the right to live in the community.

(2) The appropriate Government shall endeavour that the persons with disabilities are,—

    (a) not obliged to live in any particular living arrangement; and

    (b) given access to a range of in-house, residential and other community support services, including personal assistance necessary to support living with due regard to age and gender.

4. Protection from cruelty and inhuman treatment.

(1) The appropriate Government shall take measures to protect persons with disabilities from being subjected to torture, cruel, inhuman or degrading treatment.

(2) No person with disability shall be a subject of any research without,—

    (i) his or her free and informed consent obtained through accessible modes, means and formats of communication; and

    (ii) prior permission of a Committee for Research on Disability constituted in the prescribed manner for the purpose by the appropriate Government in which not less than half of the Members shall themselves be either persons with disabilities or Members of the registered organisation as defined under clause (z) of section 2.

5. Protection from abuse, violence and exploitation.

(1) The appropriate Government shall take measures to protect persons with disabilities from all forms of abuse, violence and exploitation and to prevent the same, shall—

    (a) take cognizance of incidents of abuse, violence and exploitation and provide legal remedies available against such incidents;

    (b) take steps for avoiding such incidents and prescribe the procedure for its reporting;

    (c) take steps to rescue, protect and rehabilitate victims of such incidents; and

    (d) create awareness and make available information among the public.

(2) Any person or registered organisation who or which has reason to believe that an act of abuse, violence or exploitation has been, or is being, or is likely to be committed against any person with disability, may give information about it to the Executive Magistrate within the local limits of whose jurisdiction such incidents occur.

(3) The Executive Magistrate on receipt of such information, shall take immediate steps to stop or prevent its occurrence, as the case may be, or pass such order as he deems fit for the protection of such person with disability including an order—

(a) to rescue the victim of such act, authorising the police or any organisation working for persons with disabilities to provide for the safe custody or rehabilitation of such person, or both, as the case may be;

(b) for providing protective custody to the person with disability, if such person so desires;

(c) to provide maintenance to such person with disability.

(4) Any police officer who receives a complaint or otherwise comes to know of abuse, violence or exploitation towards any person with disability shall inform the aggrieved person of—

(a) his or her right to apply for protection under sub-section (2) and the particulars of the Executive Magistrate having jurisdiction to provide assistance;

(b) the particulars of the nearest organisation or institution working for the rehabilitation of persons with disabilities;

(c) the right to free legal aid; and

(d) the right to file a complaint under the provisions of this Act or any other law dealing with such offence:

Provided that nothing in this section shall be construed in any manner as to relieve the police officer from his duty to proceed in accordance with law upon receipt of information as to the commission of a cognizable offence.

(5) If the Executive Magistrate finds that the alleged act or behaviour constitutes an offence under the Indian Penal Code (45 of 1860), or

under any other law for the time being in force, he may forward the complaint to that effect to the Judicial or Metropolitan Magistrate, as the case may be, having jurisdiction in the matter.

6. **Protection and safety.**

(1) The persons with disabilities shall have equal protection and safety in situations of risk, armed conflict, humanitarian emergencies and natural disasters.

(2) The National Disaster Management Authority and the State Disaster Management Authority shall take appropriate measures to ensure inclusion of persons with disabilities in its disaster management activities as defined under clause (*e*) of section 2 of the Disaster Management Act, 2005 (53 of 2005) for the safety and protection of persons with disabilities.

(3) The District Disaster Management Authority constituted under section 25 of the Disaster Management Act, 2005 (53 of 2005) shall maintain record of details of persons with disabilities in the district and take suitable measures to inform such persons of any situations of risk so as to enhance disaster preparedness.

(4) The authorities engaged in reconstruction activities subsequent to any situation of risk, armed conflict or natural disasters shall undertake such activities, in consultation with the concerned State Commissioner, in accordance with the accessibility requirements of persons with disabilities.

7. **Home and family.**

(1) No child with disability shall be separated from his or her parents on the ground of disability except on an order of competent court, if required, in the best interest of the child.

(2) Where the parents are unable to take care of a child with disability, the competent court shall place such child with his or her near relations, and failing that within the community in a family setting or in exceptional cases in shelter home run by the appropriate Government or non-governmental organisation, as may be required.

8.   Reproductive rights.

(1)   The appropriate Government shall ensure that persons with disabilities have access to appropriate information regarding reproductive and family planning.

(2)   No person with disability shall be subject to any medical procedure which leads to infertility without his or her free and informed consent.

9.   Accessibility in voting.—The Election Commission of India and the State Election Commissions shall ensure that all polling stations are accessible to persons with disabilities and all materials related to the electoral process are easily understandable by and accessible to them.

10.   Access to justice.

(1)   The appropriate Government shall ensure that persons with disabilities are able to exercise the right to access any court, tribunal, authority, commission or any other body having judicial or quasi-judicial or investigative powers without discrimination on the basis of disability.

(2)   The appropriate Government shall take steps to put in place suitable support measures for persons with disabilities specially those living outside family and those disabled requiring high support for exercising legal rights.

(3)   The National Legal Services Authority and the State Legal Services Authorities constituted under the Legal Services Authorities Act, 1987 (39 of 1987) shall make provisions including reasonable accommodation to ensure that persons with disabilities have access to any scheme, programme, facility or service offered by them equally with others.

(4)   The appropriate Government shall take steps to—

(a)   ensure that all their public documents are in accessible formats;

(b)   ensure that the filing departments, registry or any other office of records are supplied with necessary equipment to enable filing, storing and referring to the documents and evidence in accessible formats; and

(c) make available all necessary facilities and equipment to facilitate recording of testimonies, arguments or opinion given by persons with disabilities in their preferred language and means of communication.

11. Legal capacity.

(1) The appropriate Government shall ensure that the persons with disabilities have right, equally with others, to own or inherit property, movable or immovable, control their financial affairs and have access to bank loans, mortgages and other forms of financial credit.

(2) The appropriate Government shall ensure that the persons with disabilities enjoy legal capacity on an equal basis with others in all aspects of life and have the right to equal recognition everywhere as any other person before the law.

(3) When a conflict of interest arises between a person providing support and a person with disability in a particular financial, property or other economic transaction, then such supporting person shall abstain from providing support to the person with disability in that transaction:

Provided that there shall not be a presumption of conflict of interest just on the basis that the supporting person is related to the person with disability by blood, affinity or adoption.

(4) A person with disability may alter, modify or dismantle any support arrangement and seek the support of another:

Provided that such alteration, modification or dismantling shall be prospective in nature and shall not nullify any third party transaction entered into by the person with disability with the aforesaid support arrangement.

(5) Any person providing support to the person with disability shall not exercise undue influence and shall respect his or her autonomy, dignity and privacy.

12. Provision for guardianship.

(1) Notwithstanding anything contained in any other law for the time being in force, on and from the date of commencement of this Act,

where a district court or any designated authority, as notified by the State Government, finds that a person with disability, who had been provided adequate and appropriate support but is unable to take legally binding decisions, may be provided further support of a limited guardian to take legally binding decisions on his behalf in consultation with such person, in such manner, as may be prescribed by the State Government:

Provided that the District Court or the designated authority, as the case may be, may grant total support to the person with disability requiring such support or where the limited guardianship is to be granted repeatedly, in which case, the decision regarding the support to be provided shall be reviewed by the Court or the designated authority, as the case may be, to determine the nature and manner of support to be provided.

Explanation.—For the purposes of this sub-section, "limited guardianship" means a system of joint decision which operates on mutual understanding and trust between the guardian and the person with disability, which shall be limited to a specific period and for specific decision and situation and shall operate in accordance to the will of the person with disability.

(2) On and from the date of commencement of this Act, every guardian appointed under any provision of any other law for the time being in force, for a person with disability shall be deemed to function as a limited guardian.

(3) Any person with disability aggrieved by the decision of the designated authority appointing a legal guardian may prefer an appeal to such appellate authority, as may be notified by the State Government for the purpose.

13. Designation of authorities to support.

(1) The appropriate Government shall designate one or more authorities to mobilise the community and create social awareness to support persons with disabilities in exercise of their legal capacity.

(2) The authority designated under sub-section (*1*) shall take measures for setting up suitable support arrangements to exercise legal capacity by persons with disabilities living in institutions and those with high support needs and any other measures as may be required.

CHAPTER III EDUCATION

14. **Duty of educational institutions.**—The appropriate Government and the local authorities shall endeavour that all educational institutions funded or recognised by them provide inclusive education to the children with disabilities and towards that end shall—

(i) admit them without discrimination and provide education and opportunities for sports and recreation activities equally with others;

(ii) make building, campus and various facilities accessible;

(iii) provide reasonable accommodation according to the individual's requirements;

(iv) provide necessary support individualised or otherwise in environments that maximise academic and social development consistent with the goal of full inclusion;

(v) ensure that the education to persons who are blind or deaf or both is imparted in the most appropriate languages and modes and means of communication;

(vi) detect specific learning disabilities in children at the earliest and take suitable pedagogical and other measures to overcome them;

(vii) monitor participation, progress in terms of attainment levels and completion of education in respect of every student with disability;

(viii) provide transportation facilities to the children with disabilities and also the attendant of the children with disabilities having high support needs.

15. Specific measures to promote and facilitate inclusive education.—The appropriate Government and the local authorities shall take the following measures for the purpose of section 16, namely:—

(a) to conduct survey of school going children in every five years for identifying children with disabilities, ascertaining their special needs and the extent to which these are being met:

Provided that the first survey shall be conducted within a period of two years from the date of commencement of this Act;

(b) to establish adequate number of teacher training institutions;

(c) to train and employ teachers, including teachers with disability who are qualified in sign language and Braille and also teachers who are trained in teaching children with intellectual disability;

(d) to train professionals and staff to support inclusive education at all levels of school education;

(e) to establish adequate number of resource centres to support educational institutions at all levels of school education;

(f) to promote the use of appropriate augmentative and alternative modes including means and formats of communication, Braille and sign language to supplement the use of one's own speech to fulfil the daily communication needs of persons with speech, communication or language disabilities and enables them to participate and contribute to their community and society;

(g) to provide books, other learning materials and appropriate assistive devices to students with benchmark disabilities free of cost up to the age of eighteen years;

(h) to provide scholarships in appropriate cases to students with benchmark disability;

(i) to make suitable modifications in the curriculum and examination system to meet the needs of students with disabilities such as extra time for completion of examination paper, facility of scribe or amanuensis, exemption from second and third language courses;

(j) to promote research to improve learning; and

(k) any other measures, as may be required.

16. **Adult education.**—The appropriate Government and the local authorities shall take measures to promote, protect and ensure participation of persons with disabilities in adult education and continuing education programmes equally with others.

CHAPTER IV: SKILL DEVELOPMENT AND EMPLOYMENT

17. **Vocational training and self-employment.**

(1) The appropriate Government shall formulate schemes and programmes including provision of loans at concessional rates to facilitate and support employment of persons with disabilities especially for their vocational training and self-employment.

(2) The schemes and programmes referred to in sub-section (*1*) shall provide for—

    (a) inclusion of person with disability in all mainstream formal and non-formal vocational and skill training schemes and programmes;

    (b) to ensure that a person with disability has adequate support and facilities to avail specific training;

    (c) exclusive skill training programmes for persons with disabilities with active links with the market, for those with developmental, intellectual, multiple disabilities and autism;

    (d) loans at concessional rates including that of microcredit;

    (e) marketing the products made by persons with disabilities; and

    (f) maintenance of disaggregated data on the progress made in the skill training and self- employment, including persons with disabilities.

18. **Non-discrimination in employment.**

(1) No Government establishment shall discriminate against any person with disability in any matter relating to employment:
Provided that the appropriate Government may, having regard to the type of work carried on in any establishment, by notification and subject to such conditions, if any, exempt any establishment from the provisions of this section.

(2) Every Government establishment shall provide reasonable accommodation and appropriate barrier free and conducive environment to employees with disability.

(3) No promotion shall be denied to a person merely on the ground of disability.

(4) No Government establishment shall dispense with or reduce in rank, an employee who acquires a disability during his or her service:

Provided that, if an employee after acquiring disability is not suitable for the post he was holding, shall be shifted to some other post with the same pay scale and service benefits:

Provided further that if it is not possible to adjust the employee against any post, he may be kept on a supernumerary post until a suitable post is available or he attains the age of superannuation, whichever is earlier.

(5) The appropriate Government may frame policies for posting and transfer of employees with disabilities.

19. Equal opportunity policy.

(1) Every establishment shall notify equal opportunity policy detailing measures proposed to be taken by it in pursuance of the provisions of this Chapter in the manner as may be prescribed by the Central Government.

(2) Every establishment shall register a copy of the said policy with the Chief Commissioner or the State Commissioner, as the case may be.

20. Maintenance of records.

(1) Every establishment shall maintain records of the persons with disabilities in relation to the matter of employment, facilities provided and other necessary information in compliance with the provisions of this Chapter in such form and manner as may be prescribed by the Central Government.

(2) Every employment exchange shall maintain records of persons with disabilities seeking employment.

(3) The records maintained under sub-section (*1*) shall be open to inspection at all reasonable hours by such persons as may be authorised in their behalf by the appropriate Government.

21. Appointment of Grievance Redressal Officer.

(1) Every Government establishment shall appoint a Grievance Redressal Officer for the purpose of section 19 and shall inform the Chief Commissioner or the State Commissioner, as the case may be, about the appointment of such officer.

(2) Any person aggrieved with the non-compliance of the provisions of section 20, may file a complaint with the Grievance Redressal Officer, who shall investigate it and shall take up the matter with the establishment for corrective action.

(3) The Grievance Redressal Officer shall maintain a register of complaints in the manner as may be prescribed by the Central Government, and every complaint shall be inquired within two weeks of its registration.

(4) If the aggrieved person is not satisfied with the action taken on his or her complaint, he or she may approach the District-Level Committee on disability.

CHAPTER V: SOCIAL SECURITY, HEALTH, REHABILI-TATION AND RECREATION

22. Social security.

(1) The appropriate Government shall within the limit of its economic capacity and development formulate necessary schemes and programmes to safeguard and promote the right of persons with disabilities for adequate standard of living to enable them to live independently or in the community:

Provided that the quantum of assistance to the persons with disabilities under such schemes and programmes shall be at least twenty-five per cent. higher than the similar schemes applicable to others.

(2) The appropriate Government while devising these schemes and programmes shall give due consideration to the diversity of disability, gender, age, and socio-economic status.

(3) The schemes under sub-section (*1*) shall provide for,—

(a) community centres with good living conditions in terms of safety, sanitation, health care and counselling;

(b) facilities for persons including children with disabilities who have no family or have been abandoned, or are without shelter or livelihood;

(c) support during natural or man-made disasters and in areas of conflict;

(d) support to women with disability for livelihood and for upbringing of their children;

(e) access to safe drinking water and appropriate and accessible sanitation facilities especially in urban slums and rural areas;

(f) provisions of aids and appliances, medicine and diagnostic services and corrective surgery free of cost to persons with disabilities with such income ceiling as may be notified;

(g) disability pension to persons with disabilities subject to such income ceiling as may be notified;

(h) unemployment allowance to persons with disabilities registered with Special Employment Exchange for more than two years and who could not be placed in any gainful occupation;

(i) care-giver allowance to persons with disabilities with high support needs;

(j) comprehensive insurance scheme for persons with disability, not covered under the Employees State Insurance Schemes, or any other statutory or Government-sponsored insurance schemes;

(k) any other matter which the appropriate Government may think fit.

23. Healthcare.

(1) The appropriate Government and the local authorities shall take necessary measures for the persons with disabilities to provide,—

    (a) free healthcare in the vicinity specially in rural area subject to such family income as may be notified;

    (b) barrier-free access in all parts of Government and private hospitals and other healthcare institutions and centres;

    (c) priority in attendance and treatment.

(2) The appropriate Government and the local authorities shall take measures and make schemes or programmes to promote healthcare and prevent the occurrence of disabilities and for the said purpose shall—

    (a) undertake or cause to be undertaken surveys, investigations and research concerning the cause of occurrence of disabilities;

    (b) promote various methods for preventing disabilities;

    (c) screen all the children at least once in a year for the purpose of identifying "at-risk" cases;

    (d) provide facilities for training to the staff at the primary health centres;

    (e) sponsor or cause to be sponsored awareness campaigns and disseminate or cause to be disseminated information for general hygiene, health and sanitation;

    (f) take measures for pre-natal, perinatal and post-natal care of mother and child;

    (g) educate the public through the pre-schools, schools, primary health centres, village level workers and *anganwadi* workers;

    (h) create awareness amongst the masses through television, radio and other mass media on the causes of disabilities and the preventive measures to be adopted;

    (i) healthcare during the time of natural disasters and other situations of risk;

    (j) essential medical facilities for life saving emergency treatment and procedures; and

> (k) sexual and reproductive healthcare especially for women with disability.

24. Insurance schemes.—The appropriate Government shall, by notification, make insurance schemes for their employees with disabilities.

25. Rehabilitation.

(1) The appropriate Government and the local authorities shall within their economic capacity and development, undertake or cause to be undertaken services and programmes of rehabilitation, particularly in the areas of health, education and employment for all persons with disabilities.

(2) For the purposes of sub-section (*1*), the appropriate Government and the local authorities may grant financial assistance to non-Governmental Organisations.

(3) The appropriate Government and the local authorities, while formulating rehabilitation policies shall consult the non-Governmental Organisations working for the cause of persons with disabilities.

26. Research and development.—The appropriate Government shall initiate or cause to be initiated research and development through individuals and institutions on issues which shall enhance habilitation and rehabilitation and on such other issues which are necessary for the empowerment of persons with disabilities.

27. Culture and recreation.—The appropriate Government and the local authorities shall take measures to promote and protect the rights of all persons with disabilities to have a cultural life and to participate in recreational activities equally with others which include,—

(a) facilities, support and sponsorships to artists and writers with disability to pursue their interests and talents;

(b) establishment of a disability history museum which chronicles and interprets the historical experiences of persons with disabilities;

(c) making art accessible to persons with disabilities;

(d) promoting recreation centres, and other associational activities;

(e) facilitating participation in scouting, dancing, art classes, outdoor camps and adventure activities;

(f) redesigning courses in cultural and arts subjects to enable participation and access for persons with disabilities;

(g) developing technology, assistive devices and equipments to facilitate access and inclusion for persons with disabilities in recreational activities; and

(h) ensuring that persons with hearing impairment can have access to television programmes with sign language interpretation or sub-titles.

28. Sporting activities.

(1) The appropriate Government shall take measures to ensure effective participation in sporting activities of the persons with disabilities.

(2) The sports authorities shall accord due recognition to the right of persons with disabilities to participate in sports and shall make due provisions for the inclusion of persons with disabilities in their schemes and programmes for the promotion and development of sporting talents.

(3) Without prejudice to the provisions contained in sub-sections (*1*) and (*2*), the appropriate Government and the sports authorities shall take measures to,—

(a) restructure courses and programmes to ensure access, inclusion and participation of persons with disabilities in all sporting activities;

(b) redesign and support infrastructure facilities of all sporting activities for persons with disabilities;

(c) develop technology to enhance potential, talent, capacity and ability in sporting activities of all persons with disabilities;

(d) provide multi-sensory essentials and features in all sporting activities to ensure effective participation of all persons with disabilities;

(e)   allocate funds for development of state of art sport facilities for training of persons with disabilities;

(f)   promote and organise disability specific sporting events for persons with disabilities and also facilitate awards to the winners and other participants of such sporting events.

CHAPTER VI: SPECIAL PROVISIONS FOR PERSONS WITH BENCHMARK DISABILITES

29.   Free education for children with benchmark disabilities.

(1)   Notwithstanding anything contained in the Rights of Children to Free and Compulsory Education Act, 2009 (35 of 2009), every child with benchmark disability between the age of six to eighteen years shall have the right to free education in a neighbourhood school, or in a special school, of his choice.

(2)   The appropriate Government and local authorities shall ensure that every child with benchmark disability has access to free education in an appropriate environment till he attains the age of eighteen years.

30.   Reservation in higher educational institutions.

(1)   All Government institutions of higher education and other higher education institutions receiving aid from the Government shall reserve not less than five per cent. seats for persons with benchmark disabilities.

(2)   The persons with benchmark disabilities shall be given an upper age relaxation of five years for admission in institutions of higher education.

31.   Identification of posts for reservation.—The appropriate Government shall—

(i)   identify posts in the establishments which can be held by respective category of persons with benchmark disabilities in respect of the vacancies reserved in accordance with the provisions of section 34;

(ii) constitute an expert committee with representation of persons with benchmark disabilities for identification of such posts; and

(iii) undertake periodic review of the identified posts at an interval not exceeding three years.

32. Reservation.

(1) Every appropriate Government shall appoint in every Government establishment, not less than four per cent. of the total number of vacancies in the cadre strength in each group of posts meant to be filled with persons with benchmark disabilities of which, one per cent. each shall be reserved for persons with benchmark disabilities under clauses (*a*), (*b*) and (*c*) and one per cent. for persons with benchmark disabilities under clauses (*d*) and (*e*), namely:—

(a) blindness and low vision;

(b) deaf and hard of hearing;

(c) locomotor disability including cerebral palsy, leprosy cured, dwarfism, acid attack victims and muscular dystrophy;

(d) autism, intellectual disability, specific learning disability and mental illness;

(e) multiple disabilities from amongst persons under clauses (*a*) to (*d*) including deaf-blindness in the posts identified for each disabilities:

Provided that the reservation in promotion shall be in accordance with such instructions as are issued by the appropriate Government from time to time:

Provided further that the appropriate Government, in consultation with the Chief Commissioner or the State Commissioner, as the case may be, may, having regard to the type of work carried out in any Government establishment, by notification and subject to such conditions, if any, as may be specified in such notifications exempt any Government establishment from the provisions of this section.

(2) Where in any recruitment year any vacancy cannot be filled up due to non-availability of a suitable person with benchmark disability or for any other sufficient reasons, such vacancy shall be carried forward in the succeeding recruitment year and if in the succeeding recruitment year also suitable person with benchmark disability is not available, it may first be filled by interchange among the five categories and only when there is no person with disability available for the post in that year, the employer shall fill up the vacancy by appointment of a person, other than a person with disability:

Provided that if the nature of vacancies in an establishment is such that a given category of person cannot be employed, the vacancies may be interchanged among the five categories with the prior approval of the appropriate Government.

(3) The appropriate Government may, by notification, provide for such relaxation of upper age limit for employment of persons with benchmark disability, as it thinks fit.

33. Incentives to employers in private sector.—The appropriate Government and the local authorities shall, within the limit of their economic capacity and development, provide incentives to employer in private sector to ensure that at least five per cent. of their work force is composed of persons with benchmark disability.

34. Special employment exchange.—The appropriate Government may, by notification, require that from such date, the employer in every establishment shall furnish such information or return as may be prescribed by the Central Government in relation to vacancies appointed for persons with benchmark disability that have occurred or are about to occur in that establishment to such special employment exchange as may be notified by the Central Government and the establishment shall thereupon comply with such requisition.

35. **Special schemes and development programmes.**—The appropriate Government and the local authorities shall, by notification, make schemes in favour of persons with benchmark disabilities, to provide,—

   (a) five per cent. reservation in allotment of agricultural land and housing in all relevant schemes and development programmes, with appropriate priority to women with benchmark disabilities;

   (b) five per cent. reservation in all poverty alleviation and various developmental schemes with priority to women with benchmark disabilities;

   (c) five per cent. reservation in allotment of land on concessional rate, where such land is to be used for the purpose of promoting housing, shelter, setting up of occupation, business, enterprise, recreation centres and production centres.

CHAPTER VII: SPECIAL PROVISIONS FOR PERSONS WITH DISABILITIES WITH HIGH SUPPORT NEEDS

36. **Special provisions for persons with disabilities with high support.**

(1) Any person with benchmark disability, who considers himself to be in need of high support, or any person or organisation on his or her behalf, may apply to an authority, to be notified by the appropriate Government, requesting to provide high support.

(2) On receipt of an application under sub-section (*1*), the authority shall refer it to an Assessment Board consisting of such Members as may be prescribed by the Central Government.

(3) The Assessment Board shall assess the case referred to it under sub-section (*1*) in such manner as may be prescribed by the Central Government, and shall send a report to the authority certifying the need of high support and its nature.

(4) On receipt of a report under sub-section (*3*), the authority shall take steps to provide support in accordance with the report and subject to relevant schemes and orders of the appropriate Government in this behalf.

CHAPTER VIII: DUTIES AND RESPONSIBILITIES OF APPROPRIATE GOVERNMENTS

37. Awareness campaigns.

(1) The appropriate Government, in consultation with the Chief Commissioner or the State Commissioner, as the case may be, shall conduct, encourage, support or promote awareness campaigns and sensitisation programmes to ensure that the rights of the persons with disabilities provided under this Act are protected.

(2) The programmes and campaigns specified under sub-section (*1*) shall also,—

    (a) promote values of inclusion, tolerance, empathy and respect for diversity;

    (b) advance recognition of the skills, merits and abilities of persons with disabilities and of their contributions to the workforce, labour market and professional fee;

    (c) foster respect for the decisions made by persons with disabilities on all matters related to family life, relationships, bearing and raising children;

    (d) provide orientation and sensitisation at the school, college, University and professional training level on the human condition of disability and the rights of persons with disabilities;

    (e) provide orientation and sensitisation on disabling conditions and rights of persons with disabilities to employers, administrators and co-workers;

    (f) ensure that the rights of persons with disabilities are included in the curriculum in Universities, colleges and schools.

38. Accessibility.—The Central Government shall, in consultation with the Chief Commissioner, formulate rules for persons with disabilities laying down the standards of accessibility for the physical environment, transportation, information and communications, including appropriate technologies and systems, and other facilities and services provided to the public in urban and rural areas.

39. Access to transport.

(1) The appropriate Government shall take suitable measures to provide,—

(a) facilities for persons with disabilities at bus stops, railway stations and airports conforming to the accessibility standards relating to parking spaces, toilets, ticketing counters and ticketing machines;

(b) access to all modes of transport that conform the design standards, including retrofitting old modes of transport, wherever technically feasible and safe for persons with disabilities, economically viable and without entailing major structural changes in design;

(c) accessible roads to address mobility necessary for persons with disabilities.

(2) The appropriate Government shall develop schemes programmes to promote the personal mobility of persons with disabilities at affordable cost to provide for,—

(a) incentives and concessions;

(b) retrofitting of vehicles; and

(c) personal mobility assistance.

40. Access to information and communication technology.—The appropriate Government shall take measures to ensure that,—

(i) all contents available in audio, print and electronic media are in accessible format;

(ii) persons with disabilities have access to electronic media by providing audio description, sign language interpretation and close captioning;

(iii) electronic goods and equipment which are meant for every day use are available in universal design.

41. Consumer goods.—The appropriate Government shall take measures to promote development, production and distribution of universally designed consumer products and accessories for general use for persons with disabilities.

42. Mandatory observance of accessibility norms.

(1) No establishment shall be granted permission to build any structure if the building plan does not adhere to the rules formulated by the Central Government under section 40.

(2) No establishment shall be issued a certificate of completion or allowed to take occupation of a building unless it has adhered to the rules formulated by the Central Government.

43. Time limit for making existing infrastructure and premises accessible and action for that purpose.

(1) All existing public buildings shall be made accessible in accordance with the rules formulated by the Central Government within a period not exceeding five years from the date of notification of such rules:

Provided that the Central Government may grant extension of time to the States on a case to case basis for adherence to this provision depending on their state of preparedness and other related parameters.

(2) The appropriate Government and the local authorities shall formulate and publish an action plan based on prioritisation, for providing accessibility in all their buildings and spaces providing essential services such as all primary health centres, civil hospitals, schools, railway stations and bus stops.

44. Time limit for accessibility by service providers.—The service providers whether Government or private shall provide services in accordance with the rules on accessibility formulated by the Central Government under section 40 within a period of two years from the date of notification of such rules:

Provided that the Central Government in consultation with the Chief Commissioner may grant extension of time for providing certain category of services in accordance with the said rules.

45. Human resource development.

(1) Without prejudice to any function and power of Rehabilitation Council of India constituted under the Rehabilitation Council of India Act, 1992 (34 of 1992), the appropriate Government shall

endeavour to develop human resource for the purposes of this Act and to that end shall,—

(a) mandate training on disability rights in all courses for the training of Panchayati Raj Members, legislators, administrators, police officials, judges and lawyers;

(b) induct disability as a component for all education courses for schools, colleges and University teachers, doctors, nurses, para-medical personnel, social welfare officers, rural development officers, asha workers, *anganwadi* workers, engineers, architects, other professionals and community workers;

(c) initiate capacity building programmes including training in independent living and community relationships for families, members of community and other stakeholders and care providers on care giving and support;

(d) ensure independence training for persons with disabilities to build community relationships on mutual contribution and respect;

(e) conduct training programmes for sports teachers with focus on sports, games, adventure activities;

(f) any other capacity development measures as may be required.

(2) All Universities shall promote teaching and research in disability studies including establishment of study centres for such studies.

(3) In order to fulfil the obligation stated in sub-section (*1*), the appropriate Government shall in every five years undertake a need based analysis and formulate plans for the recruitment, induction, sensitisation, orientation and training of suitable personnel to undertake the various responsibilities under this Act.

46. **Social audit.**—The appropriate Government shall undertake social audit of all general schemes and programmes involving the persons with disabilities to ensure that the scheme and programmes do not have an adverse impact upon the persons with disabilities and need the requirements and concerns of persons with disabilities.

CHAPTER IX: REGISTRATION OF INSTITUTIONS FOR PERSONS WITH DISABILITIES AND GRANTS TO SUCH INSTITUTIONS

47. Competent authority.—The State Government shall appoint an authority as it deems fit to be a competent authority for the purposes of this Chapter.

48. Registration.—Save as otherwise provided under this Act, no person shall establish or maintain any institution for persons with disabilities except in accordance with a certificate of registration issued in this behalf by the competent authority:

Provided that an institution for care of mentally ill persons, which holds a valid licence under section 8 of the Mental Health Act, 1987 (14 of 1987) or any other Act for the time being in force, shall not be required to be registered under this Act.

49. Application and grant of certificate of registration.

(1) Every application for a certificate of registration shall be made to the competent authority in such form and in such manner as may be prescribed by the State Government.

(2) On receipt of an application under sub-section (*1*), the competent authority shall make such enquiries as it may deem fit and on being satisfied that the applicant has complied with the requirements of this Act and the rules made thereunder, it shall grant a certificate of registration to the applicant within a period of ninety days of receipt of application and if not satisfied, the competent authority shall, by order, refuse to grant the certificate applied for:

Provided that before making any order refusing to grant a certificate, the competent authority shall give the applicant a reasonable opportunity of being heard and every order of refusal to grant a certificate shall be communicated to the applicant in writing.

(3) No certificate of registration shall be granted under sub-section (*2*) unless the institution with respect to which an application has been made is in a position to provide such facilities and meet such standards as may be prescribed by the State Government.

(4) The certificate of registration granted under sub-section (2),—

    (a) shall, unless revoked under section 52 remain in force for such period as may be prescribed by the State Government;

    (b) may be renewed from time to time for a like period; and

    (c) shall be in such form and shall be subject to such conditions as may be prescribed by the State Government.

(5) An application for renewal of a certificate of registration shall be made not less than sixty days before the expiry of the period of validity.

(6) A copy of the certificate of registration shall be displayed by the institution in a conspicuous place.

(7) Every application made under sub-section (1) or sub-section (5) shall be disposed of by the competent authority within such period as may be prescribed by the State Government.

50. Revocation of registration.

(1) The competent authority may, if it has reason to believe that the holder of a certificate of registration granted under sub-section (2) of section 51 has,—

    (a) made a statement in relation to any application for the issue or renewal of the certificate which is incorrect or false in material particulars; or

    (b) committed or has caused to be committed any breach of rules or any conditions subject to which the certificate was granted, it may, after making such inquiry, as it deems fit, by order, revoke the certificate:

Provided that no such order shall be made until an opportunity is given to the holder of the certificate to show cause as to why the certificate of registration shall not be revoked.

(2) Where a certificate of registration in respect of an institution has been revoked under sub-section (1), such institution shall cease to function from the date of such revocation:

Provided that where an appeal lies under section 53 against the order of revocation, such institution shall cease to function,—

    (a) where no appeal has been preferred immediately on the expiry of the period prescribed for the filing of such appeal; or

(b) where such appeal has been preferred, but the order of revocation has been upheld, from the date of the order of appeal.

(3) On the revocation of a certificate of registration in respect of an institution, the competent authority may direct that any person with disability who is an inmate of such institution on the date of such revocation, shall be—

(a) restored to the custody of his or her parent, spouse or lawful guardian, as the case may be; or

(b) transferred to any other institution specified by the competent authority.

(4) Every institution which holds a certificate of registration which is revoked under this section shall, immediately after such revocation, surrender such certificate to the competent authority.

51. Appeal.

(1) Any person aggrieved by the order of the competent authority refusing to grant a certificate of registration or revoking a certificate of registration may, within such period as may be prescribed by the State Government, prefer an appeal to such appellate authority, as may be notified by the State Government against such refusal or revocation.

(2) The order of the appellate authority on such appeal shall be final.

52. Act not to apply to institutions established or maintained by Central or State Government.—Nothing contained in this Chapter shall apply to an institution for persons with disabilities established or maintained by the Central Government or a State Government.

53. Assistance to registered institutions.—The appropriate Government may within the limits of their economic capacity and development, grant financial assistance to registered institutions to provide services and to implement the schemes and programmes in pursuance of the provisions of this Act.

CHAPTER X: CERTIFICATION OF SPECIFIED DISABILITIES

54. **Guidelines for assessment of specified disabilities.**—The Central Government shall notify guidelines for the purpose of assessing the extent of specified disability in a person.

55. **Designation of certifying authorities.**

(1) The appropriate Government shall designate persons, having requisite qualifications and experience, as certifying authorities, who shall be competent to issue the certificate of disability.

(2) The appropriate Government shall also notify the jurisdiction within which and the terms and conditions subject to which, the certifying authority shall perform its certification functions.

56. **Procedure for certification.**

(1) Any person with specified disability, may apply, in such manner as may be prescribed by the Central Government, to a certifying authority having jurisdiction, for issuing of a certificate of disability.

(2) On receipt of an application under sub-section (*1*), the certifying authority shall assess the disability of the concerned person in accordance with relevant guidelines notified under section 56, and shall, after such assessment, as the case may be,—

   (a) issue a certificate of disability to such person, in such form as may be prescribed by the Central Government;

   (b) inform him in writing that he has no specified disability.

(3) The certificate of disability issued under this section shall be valid across the country.

57. **Appeal against a decision of certifying authority.**

(1) Any person aggrieved with decision of the certifying authority, may appeal against such decision, within such time and in such manner as may be prescribed by the State Government, to such appellate authority as the State Government may designate for the purpose.

(2) On receipt of an appeal, the appellate authority shall decide the appeal in such manner as may be prescribed by the State Government.

CHAPTER XI: CENTRAL AND STATE ADVISORY BOARDS ON DISABILITY AND DISTRICT LEVEL COMMITTEE

58. Constitution of Central Advisory Board on Disability.

(1) The Central Government shall, by notification, constitute a body to be known as the Central Advisory Board on Disability to exercise the powers conferred on, and to perform the functions assigned to it, under this Act.

(2) The Central Advisory Board shall consist of,—

(a) the Minister in charge of Department of Disability Affairs in the Central Government, Chairperson, *ex officio*;

(b) the Minister of State in charge dealing with Department of Disability Affairs in the Ministry in the Central Government, Vice Chairperson, *ex officio*;

(c) three Members of Parliament, of whom two shall be elected by Lok Sabha and one by the Rajya Sabha, Members, *ex officio*;

(d) the Ministers in charge of Disability Affairs of all States and Administrators or Lieutenant Governors of the Union territories, Members, *ex officio*;

(e) Secretaries to the Government of India in charge of the Ministries or Departments of Disability Affairs, Social Justice and Empowerment, School Education and Literacy, and Higher Education, Women and Child Development, Expenditure, Personnel and Training, Administrative Reforms and Public Grievances, Health and Family Welfare, Rural Development, Panchayati Raj, Industrial Policy and Promotion, Urban Development, Housing and Urban Poverty Alleviation, Science and Technology, Communications and Information Technology, Legal Affairs, Public Enterprises, Youth Affairs and Sports, Road Transport and Highways and Civil Aviation, Members, *ex officio*;

(f) Secretary, National Institute of Transforming India (NITI) Aayog, Member, *ex officio*;

(g) Chairperson, Rehabilitation Council of India, Member, *ex officio*;

(h) Chairperson, National Trust for the Welfare of Persons with Autism, Cerebral Palsy, Mental Retardation and Multiple Disabilities, Member, *ex officio*;

(i) Chairman-cum-Managing Director, National Handicapped Finance Development Corporation, Member, *ex officio*;

(j) Chairman-cum-Managing Director, Artificial Limbs Manufacturing Corporation, Member, *ex officio*;

(k) Chairman, Railway Board, Member, *ex officio*;

(l) Director-General, Employment and Training, Ministry of Labour and Employment, Member, *ex officio*;

(m) Director, National Council for Educational Research and Training, Member, *ex officio*;

(n) Chairperson, National Council of Teacher Education, Member, *ex officio*;

(o) Chairperson, University Grants Commission, Member, *ex officio*;

(p) Chairperson, Medical Council of India, Member, *ex officio*;

(q) Directors of the following Institutes:—

    (i) National Institute for the Visually Handicapped, Dehradun;

    (ii) National Institute for the Mentally Handicapped, Secunderabad;

    (iii) Pandit Deen Dayal Upadhyay Institute for the Physically Handicapped, New Delhi;

    (iv) Ali Yavar Jung National Institute for the Hearing Handicapped, Mumbai;

    (v) National Institute for the Orthopaedically Handicapped, Kolkata;

    (vi) National Institute of Rehabilitation Training and Research, Cuttack;

    (vii) National Institute for Empowerment of Persons with Multiple Disabilities, Chennai;

    (viii) National Institute for Mental Health and Sciences, Bangalore;

> > (ix) Indian Sign Language Research and Training Centre, New Delhi, Members, *ex officio*;
>
> (r) Members to be nominated by the Central Government,—
>
> > (i) five Members who are experts in the field of disability and rehabilitation;
> >
> > (ii) ten Members, as far as practicable, being persons with disabilities, to represent non-Governmental Organisations concerned with disabilities or disabled persons organisations:
> >
> > Provided that out of the ten Members nominated, at least, five Members shall be women and at least one person each shall be from the Scheduled Castes and the Scheduled Tribes;
> >
> > (iii) up to three representatives of national level chambers of commerce and industry;
>
> (s) Joint Secretary to the Government of India dealing with the subject of disability policy, Member-Secretary, *ex officio*.

59. Terms and conditions of Service of members.

(1) Save as otherwise provided under this Act, a Member of the Central Advisory Board nominated under clause (*r*) of sub-section (*2*) of section 60 shall hold office for a term of three years from the date of his nomination:

Provided that such a Member shall, notwithstanding the expiration of his term, continue to hold office until his successor enters upon his office.

(2) The Central Government may, if it thinks fit, remove any Member nominated under clause (*r*) of sub-section (*2*) of section 60, before the expiry of his term of office after giving him a reasonable opportunity of showing cause against the same.

(3) A Member nominated under clause (*r*) of sub-section (*2*) of section 60 may at any time resign his office by writing under his hand addressed to the Central Government and the seat of the said Member shall thereupon becomes vacant.

(4) A casual vacancy in the Central Advisory Board shall be filled by a fresh nomination and the person nominated to fill the vacancy shall hold office only for the remainder of the term for which the Member in whose place he was so nominated.

(5) A Member nominated under sub-clause (*i*) or sub-clause (*iii*) of clause (*r*) of sub-section (*2*) of section 60 shall be eligible for renomination.

(6) The Members nominated under sub-clause (*i*) and sub-clause (*ii*) of clause (*r*) of sub-section (*2*) of section 60 shall receive such allowances as may be prescribed by the Central Government.

60. Disqualifications.

(1) No person shall be a Member of the Central Advisory Board, who—

 (a) is, or at any time has been, adjudged insolvent or has suspended payment of his debts or has compounded with his creditors, or

 (b) is of unsound mind and stands so declared by a competent court, or

 (c) is, or has been, convicted of an offence which, in the opinion of the Central Government, involves moral turpitude, or

 (d) is, or at any time has been, convicted of an offence under this Act, or

 (e) has so abused his position in the opinion of the Central Government as a Member so as to render his continuance in the office is prejudicial interests of the general public.

(2) No order of removal shall be made by the Central Government under this section unless the Member concerned has been given a reasonable opportunity of showing cause against the same.

(3) Notwithstanding anything contained in sub-section (*1*) or sub-section (*5*) of section 61, a Member who has been removed under this section shall not be eligible for renomination as a Member.

61. Vacation of seats by Members.—If a Member of the Central Advisory Board becomes subject to any of the disqualifications specified in section 62, his seat shall become vacant.

62. Meetings of the Central Advisory Board on disability.—The Central Advisory Board shall meet at least once in every six months and shall observe such rules of procedure in regard to the transaction of business at its meetings as may be prescribed.

63. Functions of Central Advisory Board on disability.

(1) Subject to the provisions of this Act, the Central Advisory Board on disability shall be the national-level consultative and advisory body on disability matters, and shall facilitate the continuous evolution of a comprehensive policy for the empowerment of persons with disabilities and the full enjoyment of rights.

(2) In particular and without prejudice to the generality of the foregoing provisions, the Central Advisory Board on disability shall perform the following functions, namely:—

    (a) advise the Central Government and the State Governments on policies, programmes, legislation and projects with respect to disability;

    (b) develop a national policy to address issues concerning persons with disabilities;

    (c) review and coordinate the activities of all Departments of the Government and other Governmental and non-Governmental Organisations which are dealing with matters relating to persons with disabilities;

    (d) take up the cause of persons with disabilities with the concerned authorities and the international organisations with a view to provide for schemes and projects for the persons with disabilities in the national plans;

    (e) recommend steps to ensure accessibility, reasonable accommodation, non-discrimination for persons with disabilities *vis-a-vis* information, services and the built environment and their participation in social life;

    (f) monitor and evaluate the impact of laws, policies and programmes to achieve full participation of persons with disabilities; and

(g)   such other functions as may be assigned from time to time by the Central Government.

64.   State Advisory Board on disability.

(1)   Every State Government shall, by notification, constitute a body to be known as the State Advisory Board on disability to exercise the powers conferred on, and to perform the function assigned to it, under this Act.

(2)   The State Advisory Board shall consist of—

(a)   the Minister in charge of the Department in the State Government dealing with disability matters, Chairperson, *ex officio*;

(b)   the Minister of State or the Deputy Minister in charge of the Department in the State Government dealing with disability matters, if any, Vice-Chairperson, *ex officio*;

(c)   secretaries to the State Government in charge of the Departments of Disability Affairs, School Education, Literacy and Higher Education, Women and Child Development, Finance, Personnel and Training, Health and Family Welfare, Rural Development, Panchayati Raj, Industrial Policy and Promotion, Labour and Employment, Urban Development, Housing and Urban Poverty Alleviation, Science and Technology, Information Technology, Public Enterprises, Youth Affairs and Sports, Road Transport and any other Department, which the State Government considers necessary, Members, *ex officio*;

(d)   three Members of the State Legislature of whom two shall be elected by the Legislative Assembly and one by the Legislative Council, if any, and where there is no Legislative Council, three Members shall be elected by the Legislative Assembly, Members, *ex officio*;

(e)   Members to be nominated by the State Government:—

(i)   five Members who are experts in the field of disability and rehabilitation;

(ii) five Members to be nominated by the State Government by rotation to represent the districts in such manner as may be prescribed:

Provided that no nomination under this sub-clause shall be made except on the recommendation of the district administration concerned;

(iii) ten persons as far as practicable, being persons with disabilities, to represent non-Governmental Organisations or associations which are concerned with disabilities:

Provided that out of the ten persons nominated under this clause, at least, five shall be women and at least one person each shall be from the Scheduled Castes and the Scheduled Tribes;

(iv) not more than three representatives of the State Chamber of Commerce and Industry;

(f) officer not below the rank of Joint Secretary in the Department dealing with disability matters in the State Government, Member-Secretary, *ex officio*.

65. Terms and conditions of service of Members.

(1) Save as otherwise provided under this Act, a Member of the State Advisory Board nominated under clause (*e*) of sub-section (*2*) of section 66, shall hold office for a term of three years from the date of his nomination:

Provided that such a Member shall, notwithstanding the expiration of his term, continue to hold office until his successor enters upon his office.

(2) The State Government may, if it thinks fit, remove any Member nominated under clause (*e*) of sub-section (*2*) of section 66, before the expiry of his term of office after giving him a reasonable opportunity of showing cause against the same.

(3) A Member nominated under clause (*e*) of sub-section (*2*) of section 66 may at any time resign his office by writing under his hand addressed to the State Government and the seat of the said Member shall thereupon become vacant.

(4) A casual vacancy in the State Advisory Board shall be filled by a fresh nomination and the person nominated to fill the vacancy shall hold office only for the remainder of the term for which the Member in whose place he was so nominated.

(5) A Member nominated under sub-clause (*i*) or sub-clause (*iii*) of clause (*e*) of sub-section (2) of section 66 shall be eligible for renomination.

(6) The Members nominated under sub-clause (*i*) and sub-clause (*ii*) of clause (*e*) of sub-section (2) of section 66 shall receive such allowances as may be prescribed by the State Government.

66. Disqualification.

(1) No person shall be a Member of the State Advisory Board, who—

 (a) is, or at any time has been, adjudged insolvent or has suspended payment of his debts or has compounded with his creditors, or

 (b) is of unsound mind and stands so declared by a competent court, or

 (c) is, or has been, convicted of an offence which, in the opinion of the State Government, involves moral turpitude, or

 (d) is, or at any time has been, convicted of an offence under this Act, or

 (e) has so abused in the opinion of the State Government his position as a Member as to render his continuance in the State Advisory Board detrimental to the interests of the general public.

(2) No order of removal shall be made by the State Government under this section unless the Member concerned has been given a reasonable opportunity of showing cause against the same.

(3) Notwithstanding anything contained in sub-section (*1*) or sub-section (5) of section 67, a Member who has been removed under this section shall not be eligible for renomination as a Member.

67. Vacation of seats.—If a Member of the State Advisory Board becomes subject to any of the disqualifications specified in section 68 his seat shall become vacant.

68. Meetings of State Advisory Board on disability.—The State Advisory Board shall meet at least once in every six months and shall observe such rules or procedure in regard to the transaction of business at its meetings as may be prescribed by the State Government.

69. Functions of State Advisory Board on disability.

(1) Subject to the provisions of this Act, the State Advisory Board shall be the State-level consultative and advisory body on disability matters, and shall facilitate the continuous evolution of a comprehensive policy for the empowerment of persons with disabilities and the full enjoyment of rights.

(2) In particular and without prejudice to the generality of the foregoing provisions, the State Advisory Board on disability shall perform the following functions, namely:—

(a) advise the State Government on policies, programmes, legislation and projects with respect to disability;

(b) develop a State policy to address issues concerning persons with disabilities;

(c) review and coordinate the activities of all Departments of the State Government and other Governmental and non-Governmental Organisations in the State which are dealing with matters relating to persons with disabilities;

(d) take up the cause of persons with disabilities with the concerned authorities and the international organisations with a view to provide for schemes and projects for the persons with disabilities in the State plans;

(e) recommend steps to ensure accessibility, reasonable accommodation, non-discrimination for persons with disabilities, services and the built environment and their participation in social life on an equal basis with others;

(f) monitor and evaluate the impact of laws, policies and programmes designed to achieve full participation of persons with disabilities; and

(g) such other functions as may be assigned from time to time by the State Government.

70. **District-level Committee on disability.**—The State Government shall constitute District-level Committee on disability to perform such functions as may be prescribed by it.

71. **Vacancies not to invalidate proceedings.**—No act or proceeding of the Central Advisory Board on disability, a State Advisory Board on disability, or a District-level Committee on disability shall be called in question on the ground merely of the existence of any vacancy in or any defect in the constitution of such Board or Committee, as the case may be.

CHAPTER XII: CHIEF COMMISSIONER AND STATE COMMISSIONER FOR PERSONS WITH DISABILITIES

72. **Appointment of Chief Commissioner and Commissioners.**

(1) The Central Government may, by notification, appoint a Chief Commissioner for Persons with Disabilities (hereinafter referred to as the "Chief Commissioner") for the purposes of this Act.

(2) The Central Government may, by notification appoint two Commissioners to assist the Chief Commissioner, of which one Commissioner shall be a persons with disability.

(3) A person shall not be qualified for appointment as the Chief Commissioner or Commissioner unless he has special knowledge or practical experience in respect of matters relating to rehabilitation.

(4) The salary and allowances payable to and other terms and conditions of service (including pension, gratuity and other retirement benefits) of the Chief Commissioner and Commissioners shall be such as may be prescribed by the Central Government.

(5) The Central Government shall determine the nature and categories of officers and other employees required to assist the Chief Commissioner in the discharge of his functions and provide the Chief Commissioner with such officers and other employees as it thinks fit.

(6) The officers and employees provided to the Chief Commissioner shall discharge their functions under the general superintendence and control of the Chief Commissioner.

(7) The salaries and allowances and other conditions of service of officers and employees shall be such as may be prescribed by the Central Government.

(8) The Chief Commissioner shall be assisted by an advisory committee comprising of not more than eleven members drawn from the experts from different disabilities in such manner as may be prescribed by the Central Government.

73. Functions of Chief Commissioner.

(1) The Chief Commissioner shall—

    (a) identify, *suo motu* or otherwise, the provisions of any law or policy, programme and procedures, which are inconsistent with this Act and recommend necessary corrective steps;

    (b) inquire, *suo motu* or otherwise, deprivation of rights of persons with disabilities and safeguards available to them in respect of matters for which the Central Government is the appropriate Government and take up the matter with appropriate authorities for corrective action;

    (c) review the safeguards provided by or under this Act or any other law for the time being in force for the protection of rights of persons with disabilities and recommend measures for their effective implementation;

    (d) review the factors that inhibit the enjoyment of rights of persons with disabilities and recommend appropriate remedial measures;

    (e) study treaties and other international instruments on the rights of persons with disabilities and make recommendations for their effective implementation;

    (f) undertake and promote research in the field of the rights of persons with disabilities;

    (g) promote awareness of the rights of persons with disabilities and the safeguards available for their protection;

(h) monitor implementation of the provisions of this Act and schemes, programmes meant for persons with disabilities;

(i) monitor utilisation of funds disbursed by the Central Government for the benefit of persons with disabilities; and

(j) perform such other functions as the Central Government may assign.

(2) The Chief Commissioner shall consult the Commissioners on any matter while discharging its functions under this Act.

74. **Action of appropriate authorities on recommendation of Chief Commissioner.**—Whenever the Chief Commissioner makes a recommendation to an authority in pursuance of clause (b) [2][of sub- section (1)] of section 75, that authority shall take necessary action on it, and inform the Chief Commissioner of the action taken within three months from the date of receipt of the recommendation:

Provided that where an authority does not accept a recommendation, it shall convey reasons for non- acceptance to the Chief Commissioner within a period of three months, and shall also inform the aggrieved person.

75. **Powers of Chief Commissioner.**

(1) The Chief Commissioner shall, for the purpose of discharging his functions under this Act, have the same powers of a civil court as are vested in a court under the Code of Civil Procedure, 1908 (5 of 1908) while trying a suit, in respect of the following matters, namely:—

(a) summoning and enforcing the attendance of witnesses;

(b) requiring the discovery and production of any documents;

(c) requisitioning any public record or copy thereof from any court or office;

(d) receiving evidence on affidavits; and

(e) issuing commissions for the examination of witnesses or documents.

---

[2] Ins. by Act 4 of 2018, s. 3 and the second Schedule (w.e.f. 5-1-2018).

(2) Every proceeding before the Chief Commissioner shall be a judicial proceeding within the meaning of sections 193 and 228 of the Indian Penal Code (45 of 1860) and the Chief Commissioner shall be deemed to be a civil court for the purposes of section 195 and Chapter XXVI of the Code of Criminal Procedure, 1973 (2 of 1974).

76. Annual and special reports by Chief Commissioner.

(1) The Chief Commissioner shall submit an annual report to the Central Government and may at any time submit special reports on any matter, which, in his opinion, is of such urgency or importance that it shall not be deferred till submission of the annual report.

(2) The Central Government shall cause the annual and the special reports of the Chief Commissioner to be laid before each House of Parliament, along with a memorandum of action taken or proposed to be taken on his recommendations and the reasons for non-acceptance the recommendations, if any.

(3) The annual and special reports shall be prepared in such form, manner and contain such details as may be prescribed by the Central Government.

2. Appointment of State Commissioner in States.

(1) The State Government may, by notification, appoint a State Commissioner for Persons with Disabilities (hereinafter referred to as the "State Commissioner") for the purposes of this Act.

(2) A person shall not be qualified for appointment as the State Commissioner unless he has special knowledge or practical experience in respect of matters relating to rehabilitation.

(3) The salary and allowances payable to and other terms and conditions of service (including pension, gratuity and other retirement benefits) of the State Commissioner shall be such as may be prescribed by the State Government.

(4) The State Government shall determine the nature and categories of officers and other employees required to assist the State Commissioner in the discharge of his functions and provide the State Commissioner with such officers and other employees as it thinks fit.

(5) The officers and employees provided to the State Commissioner shall discharge his functions under the general superintendence and control of the State Commissioner.

(6) The salaries and allowances and other conditions of service of officers and employees shall be such as may be prescribed by the State Government.

(7) The State Commissioner shall be assisted by an advisory committee comprising of not more than five members drawn from the experts in the disability sector in such manner as may be prescribed by the State Government.

3. **Functions of State Commissioner.**—The State Commissioner shall—

(a) identify, *suo motu* or otherwise, provision of any law or policy, programme and procedures, which are in consistent with this Act, and recommend necessary corrective steps;

(b) inquire, *suo motu* or otherwise deprivation of rights of persons with disabilities and safeguards available to them in respect of matters for which the State Government is the appropriate Government and take up the matter with appropriate authorities for corrective action;

(c) review the safeguards provided by or under this Act or any other law for the time being in force for the protection of rights of persons with disabilities and recommend measures for their effective implementation;

(d) review the factors that inhibit the enjoyment of rights of persons with disabilities and recommend appropriate remedial measures;

(e) undertake and promote research in the field of the rights of persons with disabilities;

(f) promote awareness of the rights of persons with disabilities and the safeguards available for their protection;

(g) monitor implementation of the provisions of this Act and schemes, programmes meant for persons with disabilities;

(h) monitor utilisation of funds disbursed by the State Government for the benefits of persons with disabilities; and

(i) perform such other functions as the State Government may assign.

4. **Action by appropriate authorities on recommendation of State Commissioner.**—Whenever the State Commissioner makes a recommendation to an authority in pursuance of clause (*b*) of section 80, that authority shall take necessary action on it, and inform the State Commissioner of the action taken within three months from the date of receipt of the recommendation:

    Provided that where an authority does not accept a recommendation, it shall convey reasons for non- acceptance to the State Commissioner for Persons with Disabilities within the period of three months, and shall also inform the aggrieved person.

5. **Powers of State Commissioner.**

(1) The State Commissioner shall, for the purpose of discharging their functions under this Act, have the same powers of a civil court as are vested in a court under the Code of Civil Procedure, 1908 (5 of 1908) while trying a suit, in respect of the following matters, namely:—

    (a) summoning and enforcing the attendance of witnesses;

    (b) requiring the discovery and production of any documents;

    (c) requisitioning any public record or copy thereof from any court or office;

    (d) receiving evidence on affidavits; and

    (e) issuing commissions for the examination of witnesses or documents.

(2) Every proceeding before the State Commissioner shall be a judicial proceeding within the meaning of sections 193 and 228 of the Indian Penal Code (45 of 1860) and the State Commissioners shall be deemed to be a civil court for the purposes of section 195 and Chapter XXVI of the Code of Criminal Procedure, 1973 (2 of 1974).

6. **Annual and special reports by State Commissioner.**

(1) The State Commissioner shall submit an annual report to the State Government and may at any time submit special reports on any matter, which, in its opinion, is of such urgency or importance that it shall not be deferred till submission of the annual report.

(2) The State Government shall cause the annual and the special reports of the State Commissioner for persons with disabilities to be laid before each House of State Legislature where it consists of two Houses or where such Legislature consist of one House, before that House along with a memorandum of action taken or proposed to be taken on the recommendation of the State Commissioner and the reasons for non-acceptance the recommendations, if any.

(3) The annual and special reports shall be prepared in such form, manner and contain such details as may be prescribed by the State Government.

CHAPTER XIII: SPECIAL COURT

7. **Special Court.**—For the purpose of providing speedy trial, the State Government shall, with the concurrence of the Chief Justice of the High Court, by notification, specify for each district, a Court of Session to be a Special Court to try the offences under this Act.

8. **Special Public Prosecutor.**

(1) For every Special Court, the State Government may, by notification, specify a Public Prosecutor or appoint an advocate, who has been in practice as an advocate for not less than seven years, as a Special Public Prosecutor for the purpose of conducting cases in that Court.

(2) The Special Public Prosecutor appointed under sub-section (*1*) shall be entitled to receive such fees or remuneration as may be prescribed by the State Government.

CHAPTER XIV: NATIONAL FUND FOR PERSONS WITH DISABILITIES

9. **National Fund for persons with disabilities.**

(1) There shall be constituted a Fund to be called the National Fund for persons with disabilities and there shall be credited thereto—

    (a) all sums available under the Fund for people with disabilities, constituted *vide* notification No.

S.O. 573 (*E*), dated the 11th August, 1983 and the Trust Fund for Empowerment of Persons with Disabilities, constituted *vide* notification No. 30-03/2004-DDII, dated the 21st November, 2006, under the Charitable Endowment Act, 1890 (6 of 1890).

(b) all sums payable by banks, corporations, financial institutions in pursuance of judgment dated the 16th April, 2004 of the Hon'ble Supreme Court in Civil Appeal Nos. 4655 and 5218 of 2000;

(c) all sums received by way of grant, gifts, donations, benefactions, bequests or transfers;

(d) all sums received from the Central Government including grants-in-aid;

(e) all sums from such other sources as may be decided by the Central Government.

(2) The Fund for persons with disabilities shall be utilised and managed in such manner as may be prescribed.

10. Accounts and audit.

(1) The Central Government shall maintain proper accounts and other relevant records and prepare an annual statement of accounts of the Fund including the income and expenditure accounts in such form as may be prescribed in consultation with the Comptroller and Auditor-General of India.

(2) The accounts of the Fund shall be audited by the Comptroller and Auditor-General of India at such intervals as may be specified by him and any expenditure incurred by him in connection with such audit shall be payable from the Fund to the Comptroller and Auditor-General of India.

(3) The Comptroller and Auditor-General of India and any other person appointed by him in connection with the audit of the accounts of the Fund shall have the same rights, privileges and authority in connection with such audit as the Comptroller and Auditor-General of India generally has in connection with the audit of the Government accounts, and in particular, shall have the right to demand production of books of account, connected vouchers

and other documents and papers and to inspect any of the offices of the Fund.

(4) The accounts of the Fund as certified by the Comptroller and Auditor-General of India or any other person appointed by him in this behalf, together with the audit report thereon, shall be laid before each House of Parliament by the Central Government.

CHAPTER XV: STATE FUND FOR PERSONS WITH DIS-ABILITIES

11. State Fund for persons with disabilities.

(1) There shall be constituted a Fund to be called the State Fund for persons with disabilities by a State Government in such manner as may be prescribed by the State Government.

(2) The State Fund for persons with disabilities shall be utilised and managed in such manner as may be prescribed by the State Government.

(3) Every State Government shall maintain proper accounts and other relevant records of the State Fund for persons with disabilities including the income and expenditure accounts in such form as may be prescribed by the State Government in consultation with the Comptroller and Auditor-General of India.

(4) The accounts of the State Fund for persons with disabilities shall be audited by the Comptroller and Auditor-General of India at such intervals as may be specified by him and any expenditure incurred by him in connection with such audit shall be payable from the State Fund to the Comptroller and Auditor-General of India.

(5) The Comptroller and Auditor-General of India and any person appointed by him in connection with the audit of the accounts of the State Fund for persons with disabilities shall have the same rights, privileges and authority in connection with such audit as the Comptroller and Auditor-General of India generally has in connection with the audit of the Government accounts, and in particular, shall have right to demand production of books of

accounts, connected vouchers and other documents and papers and to inspect any of the offices of the State Fund.

(6) The accounts of the State Fund for persons with disabilities as certified by the Comptroller and Auditor-General of India or any other person appointed by him in this behalf together with the audit report thereon shall be laid before each House of the State Legislature where it consists of two Houses or where such Legislature consists of one House before that House.

CHAPTER XVI: OFFENCES AND PENALTIES

12. **Punishment for contravention of provisions of Act or rules or regulations made thereunder.**—Any person who contravenes any of the provisions of this Act, or of any rule made thereunder shall for first contravention be punishable with fine which may extend to ten thousand rupees and for any subsequent contravention with fine which shall not be less than fifty thousand rupees but which may extend to five lakh rupees.

13. **Offences by companies.**

(1) Where an offence under this Act has been committed by a company, every person who at the time the offence was committed, was in charge of, and was responsible to, the company for the conduct of the business of the company, as well as the company, shall be deemed to be guilty of the offence and shall be liable to be proceeded against and punished accordingly:

Provided that nothing contained in this sub-section shall render any such person liable to any punishment provided in this Act, if he proves that the offence was committed without his knowledge or that he had exercised all due diligence to prevent the commission of such offence.

(2) Notwithstanding anything contained in sub-section (*1*), where an offence under this Act has been committed by a company and it is proved that the offence has been committed with the consent or connivance of, or is attributable to any neglect on the part of any

director, manager, secretary or other officer of the company, such director, manager, secretary or other officer shall also be deemed to be guilty of that offence and shall be liable to be proceeded against and punished accordingly.

Explanation.—For the purposes of this section,—

(a) "company" means any body corporate and includes a firm or other association of individuals;

and

(b) "director", in relation to a firm, means a partner in the firm.

14. **Punishment for fraudulently availing any benefit meant for persons with benchmark disabilities.**—Whoever, fraudulently avails or attempts to avail any benefit meant for persons with benchmark disabilities, shall be punishable with imprisonment for a term which may extend to two years or with fine which may extend to one lakh rupees or with both.

15. **Punishment for offences of atrocities.**—Whoever,—

(a) intentionally insults or intimidates with intent to humiliate a person with disability in any place within public view;

(b) assaults or uses force to any person with disability with intent to dishonour him or outrage the modesty of a woman with disability;

(c) having the actual charge or control over a person with disability voluntarily or knowingly denies food or fluids to him or her;

(d) being in a position to dominate the will of a child or woman with disability and uses that position to exploit her sexually;

(e) voluntarily injures, damages or interferes with the use of any limb or sense or any supporting device of a person with disability;

(f) performs, conducts or directs any medical procedure to be performed on a woman with disability which leads to or is likely to lead to termination of pregnancy without her express consent except in cases where medical procedure for termination of pregnancy is done in severe cases of disability and with the opinion of a registered medical practitioner and also with the consent of the guardian of the woman with disability, shall be punishable with imprisonment for a term which shall not be less than six months but which may extend to five years and with fine.

16. **Punishment for failure to furnish information.**—Whoever, fails to produce any book, account or other documents or to furnish any statement, information or particulars which, under this Act or any order, or direction made or given there under, is duty bound to produce or furnish or to answer any question put in pursuance of the provisions of this Act or of any order, or direction made or given thereunder, shall be punishable with fine which may extend to twenty-five thousand rupees in respect of each offence, and in case of continued failure or refusal, with further fine which may extend to one thousand rupees for each day, of continued failure or refusal after the date of original order imposing punishment of fine.

17. **Previous sanction of appropriate Government.**—No Court shall take cognizance of an offence alleged to have been committed by an employee of the appropriate Government under this Chapter, except with the previous sanction of the appropriate Government or a complaint is filed by an officer authorised by it in this behalf.

18. **Alternative punishments.**—Where an act or omission constitutes an offence punishable under this Act and also under any other Central or State Act, then, notwithstanding anything contained in any other law for the time being in force, the offender found guilty of such offence shall be liable to punishment only under such Act as provides for punishment which is greater in degree.

CHAPTER XVII: MISCELLANEOUS

19. **Application of other laws not barred.**—The provisions of this Act shall be in addition to, and not in derogation of, the provisions of any other law for the time being in force.

20. **Protection of action taken in good faith.**—No suit, prosecution or other legal proceeding shall lie against the appropriate Government

or any officer of the appropriate Government or any officer or employee of the Chief Commissioner or the State Commissioner for anything which is in good faith done or intended to be done under this Act or the rules made thereunder.

21. Power to remove difficulties.

(1) If any difficulty arises in giving effect to the provisions of this Act, the Central Government may, by order, published in the Official Gazette, make such provisions or give such directions, not inconsistent with the provisions of this Act, as may appear to it to be necessary or expedient for removing the difficulty:

Provided that no such order shall be made under this section after the expiry of the period of two years from the date of commencement of this Act.

(2) Every order made under this section shall be laid as soon as may be, after it is made, before each House of Parliament.

22. Power to amend Schedule.

(1) On the recommendations made by the appropriate Government or otherwise, if the Central Government is satisfied that it is necessary or expedient so to do, it may, by notification, amend the Schedule and any such notification being issued, the Schedule shall be deemed to have been amended accordingly.

(2) Every such notification shall, as soon as possible after it is issued, shall be laid before each House of Parliament.

23. Power of Central Government to make rules.

(1) The Central Government may, subject to the condition of previous publication, by notification, make rules for carrying out the provisions of this Act.

(2) In particular, and without prejudice to the generality of the foregoing power, such rules may provide for all or any of the following matters, namely:—

(a) the manner of constituting the Committee for Research on Disability under sub-section (2) of section 6;

(b) the manner of notifying the equal opportunity policy under sub-section (1) of section 21;

(c) the form and manner of maintaining records by every establishment under sub-section (*1*) of section 22;

(d) the manner of maintenance of register of complaints by grievance redressal officer under sub-section (*3*) of section 23;

(e) the manner of furnishing information and return by establishment to the Special Employment Exchange under section 36;

(f) the composition of the Assessment Board under sub-section (*2*) and manner of assessment to be made by the Assessment Board under sub-section (*3*) of section 38;

(g) rules for person with disabilities laying down the standards of accessibility under section 40;

(h) the manner of application for issuance of certificate of disability under sub-section (*1*) and form of certificate of disability under sub-section (*2*) of section 58;

(i) the allowances to be paid to nominated Members of the Central Advisory Board under sub-section (*6*) of section 61;

(j) the rules of procedure for transaction of business in the meetings of the Central Advisory Board under section 64;

(k) the salaries and allowances and other conditions of services of Chief Commissioner and Commissioners under sub-section (*4*) of section 74;

(l) the salaries and allowances and conditions of services of officers and staff of the Chief Commissioner under sub-section (*7*) of section 74;

(m) the composition and manner of appointment of experts in the advisory committee under sub-section (*8*) of section 74;

(n) the form, manner and content of annual report to be prepared and submitted by the Chief Commissioner under sub-section (*3*) of section 78;

(o) the procedure, manner of utilisation and management of the Fund under sub-section (*2*) of section 86; and

(p) the form for preparation of accounts of Fund under sub-section (*1*) of section 87.

(3) Every rule made under this Act shall be laid, as soon as may be after it is made, before each House of Parliament while it is in session, for a total period of thirty days which may be comprised in one session or in two or more successive sessions, and if, before the expiry of the session immediately following the session or the successive sessions aforesaid, both Houses agree in making any modification in the rule or both Houses agree that the rule should not be made, the rule shall thereafter have effect only in such modified form or be of no effect, as the case may be; so, however, that any such modification or annulment shall be without prejudice to the validity of anything previously done under that rule.

24. Power of State Government to make rules.

(1) The State Government may, subject to the condition of previous publication, by notification, make rules for carrying out the provisions of this Act, not later than six months from the date of commencement of this Act.

(2) In particular, and without prejudice to the generality of foregoing powers, such rules may provide for all or any of the following matters, namely:—

(a) the manner of constituting the Committee for Research on Disability under sub-section (2) of section 5;

(b) the manner of providing support of a limited guardian under sub-section (1) of section 14;

(c) the form and manner of making an application for certificate of registration under sub-section (1) of section 51;

(d) the facilities to be provided and standards to be met by institutions for grant of certificate of registration under sub-section (3) of section 51;

(e) the validity of certificate of registration, the form of, and conditions attached to, certificate of registration under sub-section (4) of section 51;

(f) the period of disposal of application for certificate of registration under sub-section (7) of section 51;

(g) the period within which an appeal to be made under sub-section (*1*) of section 53;

(h) the time and manner of appealing against the order of certifying authority under sub-section (*1*) and manner of disposal of such appeal under sub-section (*2*) of section 59;

(i) the allowances to be paid to nominated Members of the State Advisory Board under sub-section (*6*) of section 67;

(j) the rules of procedure for transaction of business in the meetings of the State Advisory Board under section 70;

(k) the composition and functions of District Level Committee under section 72;

(l) salaries, allowances and other conditions of services of the State Commissioner under sub-section (*3*) of section 79;

(m) the salaries, allowances and conditions of services of officers and staff of the State Commissioner under sub-section (*3*) of section 79;

(n) the composition and manner of appointment of experts in the advisory committee under sub-section (*7*) of section 79;

(o) the form, manner and content of annual and special reports to be prepared and submitted by the State Commissioner under sub-section (*3*) of section 83;

(p) the fee or remuneration to be paid to the Special Public Prosecutor under sub-section (*2*) of section 85;

(q) the manner of constitution of State Fund for persons with disabilities under sub-section (*1*), and the manner of utilisation and management of State Fund under sub-section (*2*) of section 88;

(r) the form for preparation of accounts of the State Fund for persons with disabilities under sub-section (*3*) of section 88.

(3) Every rule made by the State Government under this Act shall be laid, as soon as may be after it is made, before each House of the State Legislature where it consists of two Houses, or where such State Legislature consists of one House, before that House.

25. Repeal and savings.

(1) The Persons with Disabilities (Equal Opportunity Protection of Rights and Full Participation) Act, 1995 (1 of 1996) is hereby repealed.

(2) Notwithstanding the repeal of the said Act, anything done or any action taken under the said Act, shall be deemed to have been done or taken under the corresponding provisions of this Act.

THE SCHEDULE

[*See* clause (*zc*) of section 2] SPECIFIED DISABILITY

1. Physical disability.—

A. Locomotor disability (a person's inability to execute distinctive activities associated with movement of self and objects resulting from affliction of musculoskeletal or nervous system or both), including—

(a) "leprosy cured person" means a person who has been cured of leprosy but is suffering from—

  (i) loss of sensation in hands or feet as well as loss of sensation and paresis in the eye and eye-lid but with no manifest deformity;

  (ii) manifest deformity and paresis but having sufficient mobility in their hands and feet to enable them to engage in normal economic activity;

  (iii) extreme physical deformity as well as advanced age which prevents him/her from undertaking any gainful occupation, and the expression "leprosy cured" shall construed accordingly;

(b) "cerebral palsy" means a Group of non-progressive neurological condition affecting body movements and muscle coordination, caused by damage to one or more specific areas of the brain, usually occurring before, during or shortly after birth;

(c) "dwarfism" means a medical or genetic condition resulting in an adult height of 4 feet 10 inches (147 centimeters) or less;

(d) "muscular dystrophy" means a group of hereditary genetic muscle disease that weakens the muscles that move the human body and persons with multiple dystrophy have incorrect and missing information in their genes, which prevents them from making the proteins they need for healthy muscles. It is characterised by progressive skeletal muscle weakness, defects in muscle proteins, and the death of muscle cells and tissue;

(e) "acid attack victims" means a person disfigured due to violent assaults by throwing of acid or similar corrosive substance.

B. Visual impairment—

(a) "blindness" means a condition where a person has any of the following conditions, after best correction—

(i)   total absence of sight; or

(ii)   visual acuity less than 3/60 or less than 10/200 (Snellen) in the better eye with best possible correction; or

(iii) limitation of the field of vision subtending an angle of less than 10 degree.

(b) "low-vision" means a condition where a person has any of the following conditons, namely:—

(i)   visual acuity not exceeding 6/18 or less than 20/60 upto 3/60 or upto 10/200 (Snellen) in the better eye with best possible corrections; or

(ii)   limitation of the field of vision subtending an angle of less than 40 degree up to 10 degree.

C. Hearing impairment—

(a) "deaf" means persons having 70 DB hearing loss in speech frequencies in both ears;

(b) "hard of hearing" means person having 60 DB to 70 DB hearing loss in speech frequencies in both ears;

D. "speech and language disability" means a permanent disability arising out of conditions such as laryngectomy or aphasia affecting one or more components of speech and language due to organic or neurological causes.

2. Intellectual disability, a condition characterised by significant limitation both in intellectual functioning (rasoning, learning, problem solving) and in adaptive behaviour which covers a range of every day, social and practical skills, including—

    (a) "specific learning disabilities" means a heterogeneous group of conditions wherein there is a deficit in processing language, spoken or written, that may manifest itself as a difficulty to comprehend, speak, read, write, spell, or to do mathematical calculations and includes such conditions as perceptual disabilities, dyslexia, dysgraphia, dyscalculia, dyspraxia and developmental aphasia;

    (b) "autism spectrum disorder" means a neuro-developmental condition typically appearing in the first three years of life that significantly affects a person's ability to communicate, understand relationships and relate to others, and is frequently associated with unusal or stereotypical rituals or behaviours.

3. Mental behaviour,— "mental illness" means a substantial disorder of thinking, mood, perception, orientation or memory that grossly impairs judgment, behaviour, capacity to recognise reality or ability to meet the ordinary demands of life, but does not include retardation which is a conditon of arrested or incomplete development of mind of a person, specially characterised by subnormality of intelligence.

4. Disability caused due to—

(a) chronic neurological conditions, such as—

    (i) "multiple sclerosis" means an inflammatory, nervous system disease in which the myelin sheaths around the axons of nerve cells of the brain and spinal cord are damaged, leading to demyelination and affecting the ability of nerve cells in the brain and spinal cord to communicate with each other;

    (ii) "parkinson's disease" means a progressive disease of the nervous system marked by tremor, muscular rigidity, and slow, imprecise movement, chiefly affecting middle-aged and elderly people associated with degeneration of the basal ganglia of the brain and a deficiency of the neurotransmitter dopamine.

(b) Blood disorder—

    (i) "haemophilia" means an inheritable disease, usually affecting only male but transmitted by women to their male children, characterised by loss or impairment of the normal clotting ability of blood so that a minor would may result in fatal bleeding;

    (ii) "thalassemia" means a group of inherited disorders characterised by reduced or absent amounts of haemoglobin.

    (iii) "sickle cell disease" means a hemolytic disorder characterised by chronic anemia, painful events, and various complications due to associated tissue and organ damage; "hemolytic" refers to the destruction of the cell membrane of red blood cells resulting in the release of hemoglobin.

5. Multiple Disabilities (more than one of the above specified disabilities) including deaf blindness which means a condition in which a person may have combination of hearing and visual impairments causing severe communication, developmental, and educational problems.

6. Any other category as may be notified by the Central Government.

RPWD Rules 2017 and Amendment Rules 2019

The Rights of Persons with Disabilities Rules, 2017
Published vide Notification No. G.S.R. 591(E), dated 15th June, 2017
(Includes Insertion of Chapter V A vide the Rights of Persons with
Disabilities (Amendment) Rules, 2019 published vide notification
No. G.S.R. 209(E), dated 08th March 2019
[Department of Empowerment of Persons with Disabilities (Divyangjan)]

Ministry of Social Justice and Empowerment

G.S.R. 591(E). - Whereas a draft of the Rights of Persons with Disabilities Rules, 2017 was published as required by sub-sections (1) and (2) of section 100 of the Rights of Persons with Disabilities Act, 2016 (49 of 2016) in the Gazette of India, Extraordinary, Part-II, Section 3, Sub-section (i) *vide* number G.S.R. 398 (E), dated the 21st April, 2017, inviting objections and suggestions from all persons likely to be affected thereby, before the expiry of thirty days from the date on which the copies of the Official Gazette containing the said notification were made available to the public;

And whereas the copies of the *Official Gazette* in which the said notification was published were made available to the public on the 22nd April, 2017;

And whereas objections and suggestions received from the public on the said draft rules were considered by the Central Government;

Now, therefore, in exercise of powers conferred by sub-sections (1) and (2) of section 100 of the Rights of Persons with Disabilities Act, 2016 (49 of 2016), the Central Government hereby makes the following rules, namely:-

CHAPTER I

Preliminary

1. Short title, extent and commencement.

(1) These rules may be called the Rights of Persons with Disabilities Rules, 2017.

(2) They extend to the whole of India.

(3) They shall come into force from the date of their publication in the Official Gazette.

2. Definitions.

(1) In these rules, unless the context otherwise requires,-

    (a) *"Act"* means the Rights of Persons with Disabilities Act, 2016 (49 of 2016);

    (b) *"certificate"* means a certificate of disability issued under section 57 of the Act;

    (c) *"Form"* means a form appended to these rules.

(2) Words and expressions used herein and not defined but defined in the Act shall have the meanings respectively assigned to them in the Act.

CHAPTER II

Rights and Entitlements

3. Establishment not to discriminate on the ground of disability.

(1) The head of the establishment shall ensure that the provision of sub-section (3) of section 3 of the Act are not misused to deny any right or benefit to persons with disabilities covered under the Act.

(2) If the head of the Government establishment or a private establishment employing twenty or more persons receives a complaint from an aggrieved persons regarding discrimination on the ground of disability, he shall -

    (a) initiate action in accordance with the provisions of the Act; or

    (b) inform the aggrieved person in writing as to how the impugned act or omission is a proportionate means of achieving a legitimate aim.

(3) If the aggrieved person submits a complaint to the Chief Commissioner or State Commissioner for Persons with Disabilities, as the case may be, the complaint shall be disposed of within a period of sixty days:

Provided that in exceptional cases, the Chief Commissioner or State Commissioner may dispose of such complaint within thirty days.

(4) No establishment shall compel a person with disability to partly or fully pay the costs incurred for reasonable accommodation.

4. Central Committee for Research on Disability.

(1) The Central Committee for Research on Disability shall consist of the following persons, namely:-

    (i) an eminent person having vast experience in the field of science or medicine, to be nominated by the Central Government, *ex officio* - Chairperson;

    (ii) nominee of the Director General of Health Services not below the rank of Deputy Director General - Member;

    (iii) four persons drawn from National Institutes representing physical, visual, hearing and intellectual disabilities, to be nominated by the Central Government - Members;

    (iv) five persons as representatives of the registered organisations, from each of the five groups of specified disabilities in the Schedule to the Act, to be nominated by the Central Government - Members:

    Provided that at least one representative of the registered organizations is a woman;

    (v) the Director, Department of Empowerment of Persons with Disabilities, New Delhi shall be the Member Secretary.

(2) The Chairperson may invite any expert as a special invitee.

(3) The term of office of the nominated members shall be for a period of three years from the date on which they enter upon office, and the nominated member shall be eligible for re-nomination for one more term.

(4) One half of the members shall constitute the quorum for the meeting.

(5) The non-official members and special invitees shall be entitled for travelling allowance and daily allowance as admissible to a Group "A" officer of the Central Government.

(6) The Central Government may provide the Committee with such clerical and other staff as it deems necessary.

5. **Person with disability not to be a subject of research.** - No person with disability shall be a subject of research except when the research involves physical impact on his body.

6. **Procedure to be followed by Executive Magistrate.** - For the purposes of dealing with the complaints under section 7 of the Act, the Executive Magistrate shall follow the procedure provided in sections 133 to 143 of the Code of Criminal Procedure, 1973 (2 of 1974).

CHAPTER III

Nodal Officer in the District Education Office

7. There shall be a nodal officer in the District Education Office to deal with all matters relating to admission of children with disabilities and the facilities to be provided to them in schools in accordance with the provisions of sections 16 and 31 of the Act.

CHAPTER IV

Employment

8. **Manner of publication of equal opportunity policy.**

(1) Every establishment shall publish equal opportunity policy for persons with disabilities.

(2) The establishment shall display the equal opportunity policy preferably on their website, failing which, at conspicuous places in their premises.

(3) The equal opportunity policy of a private establishment having twenty or more employees and the Government establishments shall *inter alia*, contain the following, namely:-

 (a) facility and amenity to be provided to the persons with disabilities to enable them to effectively discharge their duties in the establishment;

(b) list of posts identified suitable for persons with disabilities in the establishment;

(c) the manner of selection of persons with disabilities for various posts, post-recruitment and pre-promotion training, preference in transfer and posting, special leave, preference in allotment of residential accommodation if any, and other facilities;

(d) provisions for assistive devices, barrier-free accessibility and other provisions for persons with disabilities;

(e) appointment of liaison officer by the establishment to look after the recruitment of persons with disabilities and provisions of facilities and amenities for such employees.

(4) The equal opportunity policy of the private establishment having less than twenty employees shall contain facilities and amenities to be provided to the persons with disabilities to enable them to effectively discharge their duties in the establishment.

9. Form and manner of maintaining records by the establishments.

(1) Every establishment covered under sub-rule (3) of rule 8 shall maintain records containing the following particulars, namely:-

(a) the number of persons with disabilities who are employed and the date from when they are employed;

(b) the name, gender and address of persons with disabilities;

(c) the nature of disability of such persons;

(d) the nature of work being rendered by such employed person with disability; and

(e) the kind of facilities being provided to such persons with disabilities.

(2) Every establishment shall produce for inspection on demand, records maintained under these rules, to the authorities under this Act and shall supply such information which may be required for the purpose of ascertaining whether the provisions have been complied with.

10. Manner of maintenance of register of complaints by the Government establishments.

(1) Every Government establishment shall appoint an officer not below the rank of a Gazetted Officer as Grievance Redressal Officer:

Provided that where it is not possible to appoint any Gazetted Officer, the Government establishment may appoint the senior most Officer as a Grievance Redressal Officer.

(2) The Grievance Redressal Officer shall maintain a register of complaints of persons with disabilities with the following particulars, namely:-

(a) date of complaint;

(b) name of complainant;

(c) name of the person who is enquiring the complaint;

(d) place of incident;

(e) the name of establishment or person against whom the complaint is made;

(f) gist of the complaint;

(g) documentary evidence, if any;

(h) date of disposal by the Grievance Redressal Officer;

(i) details of disposal of the appeal by the district level committee; and

(j) any other information.

CHAPTER V

Vacancies for Persons with Benchmark Disabilities

11. Computation of vacancies.

(1) For the purposes of computation of vacancies, four percent of the total number of vacancies including vacancies arising in the identified and non-identified posts in the cadre strength in each group of posts shall be taken into account by the appropriate Government for the persons with benchmark disabilities:

Provided that the reservation in promotion shall be in accordance with the instructions issued by the appropriate Government from time to time.

(2) Every Government establishment shall maintain a vacancy based roster for the purpose of calculation of vacancies for persons with benchmark disabilities in the cadre strength as per the instructions issued by the appropriate Government from time to time.

(3) While making advertisement to fill up vacancies, every Government establishment shall indicate the number of vacancies reserved for each class of persons with benchmark disabilities in accordance with the provisions of section 34 of the Act.

(4) The reservation for persons with disabilities in accordance with the provisions of section 34 of the Act shall be horizontal and the vacancies for persons with benchmark disabilities shall be maintained as a separate class.

12. **Interchange of vacancies.** - The Government establishment shall interchange vacancies in accordance with the provisions of section 34 of the Act, only if due process of recruitment to fill up the vacancies reserved for persons with benchmark disabilities has been complied with.

13. **Submission of Returns on Vacancies.**

(1) Every Government establishment shall furnish to the local special employment exchange returns in Form - I once in every six months for the period from 1st April to 30th September and from 1st October to 31st March, and in Form -II once in every two years.

(2) The six monthly return shall be furnished within thirty days of the respective dates which is, 31st March and, 30th September of every financial year.

(3) The two yearly return shall be furnished within thirty days of the closing of every alternate financial year:

Provided that the first two yearly returns shall be furnished for the financial year closing on 31st March, 2019.

14. **Form in which record to be kept by an employer.** - Every Government establishment shall maintain the record of employees with disabilities in Form - III.

CHAPTER V A

(Inserted vide Rights of Persons with Disabilities (Amendment) Rules, 2019)

14A. (1) The State Governments or Union Territory Administrations shall notify the authority to whom a person with benchmark disability can apply for the high support requirement as per sub-section (1) of Section 38 of the Act.

(2) Only the persons with benchmark disabilities having permanent certificate of disability shall be eligible for applying for high support requirement.

(3) The State Governments shall constitute Assessment Board at the District level or Division level based on the number of persons with benchmark disabilities comprising the following:-
   (a) District Chief Medical Officer or Civil Surgeon or Medical Superintendent …. Chairperson;
   (b) District Social Welfare Officer ……… Member;
   (c) Five rehabilitation specialists [Physical Medicine and Rehabilitation or Orthopaedic specialist, ENT specialist, Ophthalmologist, General Physician (if the applicant is 18 years or above) or Pediatrician (if the applicant is less than 18 years), Psychiatrist] …………Members;
   (d) Occupational therapist or speech therapist or Clinical Psychologist or Physiotherapist (as per requirement) …………Member;
   (e) Any other expert as the Chairperson deems appropriate ……….. Member.

(4) The authority notified under sub-rule (1) shall refer every case to the Assessment Board for assessment of applicant's high support requirement.

(5) The Assessment Board shall invite the applicant of high support requirements for assessment and may, if necessary, seek clinical assessment.

(6) The Assessment Board shall assess the applicant on the basis of the six parameters (a) to (f) and assign scores on the basis of the 100 point graded weightage indicated below:-

Parameters		Weightage
(a) Severity of physical disability (Max. weightage – 25)	(a) 40% - 59% (b) 60% - 79% (c) 80% - 100%	15 20 25
(b) Severity of mental/ developmental disability (which restricts the person to take any informed decision) (Max. weightage – 25)	(a) 40% - 59% (b) 60% - 79% (c) 80% - 100%	15 20 25
(c) The extent to which daily activities in a person is hampered (Max. weightage – 35)	(i) Bathing, Brushing, combing, Dressing (ii) Toilet hygiene (getting to the toilet, cleaning oneself, getting backup etc) (iii) Functional mobility (ability to work, get in and out of bed, get in and out of a chair, moving from one place to other while performing activities) (iv) Self-feeding (not including cooking)	10 10 10 5
(d) Cognitive Abilities like ability to take safety measures to use transport, logistics, gadgets, not to get lost (Max. weightage – 5)	-	5
(e) Environmental Barriers like access to health care or support systems for rehabilitation or health needs (Max. weightage – 5)	-	5
(f) Socio-economic status (Max. weightage – 5)	APL BPL	0 5
Total		100

(7) Any person with benchmark disability with a score 60 out of 100 point mentioned in sub-rule (6) may be recommended by the Assessment Board for high support needs.

(8) The Assessment Board shall submit its recommendations to the authority notified under sub-rule (1) within a period of 90 days from the date of receiving request for assessment from the said authority.

(9) The State Government or Union Territory Administrations may develop dedicated schemes to provide high support to such persons with benchmark disabilities.

(10) The authority notified under sub-rule (1) shall consider the application for high support requirement on the basis of the recommendations of the Assessment Board keeping in view the schemes or programmes of the respective State Governments or Union Territory Administrations, as the case may be.

CHAPTER VI

Accessibility

15. Rules for Accessibility.

(1) Every establishment shall comply with the following standards relating to physical environment, transport and information and communication technology, namely: -

(a) standard for public buildings as specified in the Harmonised Guidelines and Space Standards for Barrier Free Built Environment for Persons With Disabilities and Elderly Persons as issued by the Government of India, Ministry of Urban Development in March, 2016;

(b) standard for Bus Body Code for transportation system as specified in the notification of the Government of India in the Ministry of Road Transport and Highways, *vide* number G.S.R. 895(E), dated the 20th September, 2016;

(c) Information and Communication Technology -

(i) website standard as specified in the guidelines for Indian Government websites, as adopted by Department of Administrative Reforms and Public Grievances, Government of India;

(ii) documents to be placed on websites shall be in Electronic Publication (ePUB) or Optical Character Reader (OCR) based Pdf format:

Provided that the standard of accessibility in respect of other services and facilities shall be specified by the Central Government within a period of six months from the date of notification of these rules.

(2) The respective Ministries and Departments shall ensure compliance of the standards of accessibility specified under this rule through the concerned domain regulators or otherwise.

16. **Review of Accessibility Standards.** - The Central Government shall review from time to time the accessibility standards notified based on the latest scientific knowledge and technology.

CHAPTER VII

Certificate of Disability

17. **Application for certificate of disability.**

(1) Any person with specified disability may apply in Form -IV for a certificate of disability and submit the application to -

(a) a medical authority or any other notified competent authority to issue such a certificate in the district of residence of the applicant as mentioned in the proof of residence in the application; or

(b) the concerned medical authority in a government hospital where he may be undergoing or may have undergone treatment in connection with his disability:

Provided that where a person with disability is a minor or suffering from intellectual disability or any other disability which renders him unfit or unable to make such an application himself, the application on his behalf may be made by his legal guardian or by any organisation registered under the Act having the minor under its care.

(2) The application shall be accompanied by -

(a) proof of residence;

(b) two recent passport size photographs; and

(c) aadhaar number or aadhaar enrollment number, if any.

Note. - No other proof of residence shall be demanded from the applicant who has aadhaar or aadhaar enrollment number.

18. Issue of certificate of disability.

(1) On receipt of an application under rule 17, the medical authority or any other notified competent authority shall, verify the information as provided by the applicant and shall assess the disability in terms of the relevant guidelines issued by the Central Government and after satisfying himself that the applicant is a person with disability, issue a certificate of disability in his favour in Form V, VI and VII, as the case may be.

(2) The medical authority shall issue the certificate of disability within a month from the date of receipt of the application.

(3) The medical authority shall, after due examination -

(i) issue a permanent certificate of disability in cases where there are no chances of variation of disability over time in the degree of disability; or

(ii) issue a certificate of disability indicating the period of validity, in cases where there is any chance of variation over time in the degree of disability.

(4) If an applicant is found ineligible for issue of certificate of disability, the medical authority shall convey the reasons to him in writing under Form VIII within a period of one month from the date of receipt of the application.

(5) The State Government and Union territory Administration shall ensure that the certificate of disability is granted on online platform from such date as may be notified by the Central Government.

19. Certificate issued under rule 18 to be generally valid for all purposes. - A person to whom the certificate issued under rule 18 shall be entitled to apply for facilities, concessions and benefits admissible for persons with disabilities under schemes of the Government and of non-Governmental organizations funded by the Government.

20. **Validity of certificate of disability issued under the repealed Act.** - The certificate of disability issued under the Persons with Disabilities (Equal Opportunities, Protection of Rights and Full Participation) Act, 1995 (1 of 1996) shall continue to be valid after commencement of the Act for the period specified therein.

CHAPTER VIII

Central Advisory Board on Disability

21. **Allowances for the members of the Central Advisory Board.**

(1) The non-official members of the Central Advisory Board, in Delhi, shall be paid an allowance of rupees two thousand per day for each day of the actual meeting.

(2) The non-official members of the Central Advisory Board, not residing in Delhi shall be paid daily allowance and travelling allowance for each day of the actual meeting at the rate admissible to a Group "A" officer of the Central Government:

Provided that in case a Member of Parliament who is a Member of the Central Advisory Board, the daily allowance and travelling allowance shall be paid at the rate admissible to him as Member of Parliament when the Parliament is not in session and on production of a certificate by the Member that he has not drawn any such allowance for the same journey and halts from any other Government source.

(3) The official member of the Central Advisory Board shall be paid daily allowance and travelling allowance, at the rate admissible under the relevant rules of the respective Government under whom he is serving on production of a certificate by him that he has not drawn any such allowance for the same journey and halts from any other Government source.

22. Notice of meeting.

(1) The meeting of the Central Advisory Board on disability shall ordinarily be held in New Delhi on such dates as may be fixed by the Chairperson:

Provided that it shall meet at least once in every six months.

(2) The Chairperson shall, on the written request of not less than ten members of the Central Advisory Board, call a special meeting of the Board.

(3) The Member -Secretary shall give fifteen clear days' notice of an ordinary meeting and five clear days' notice of a special meeting specifying the time and the place at which such meeting is to be held and the business to be transacted thereat.

(4) The Member-Secretary may give notice to the members by delivering the same by messenger or sending it by registered post to his last known place of residence or business or by email or in such other manner as the Chairperson may, in the circumstances of the case, think fit.

(5) No member shall be entitled to bring forward for the consideration of the meeting, any matter of which he has not given ten clear days' notice to the Member- Secretary, unless the Chairperson may permit him to do so.

(6) The Central Advisory Board may adjourn its meeting from day to day or to any particular day.

(7) Where a meeting of the Central Advisory Board is adjourned from day to day, the Member-Secretary shall give notice of such adjourned meeting at the place where the meeting is adjourned, if held, by messenger and it shall not be necessary to give notice of the adjourned meeting to other members.

(8) Where a meeting of the Central Advisory Board is adjourned not from day to day but from the day on which the meeting is to be held to another day, notice of such meeting shall be given to all the members as provided in sub-rule (4).

23. Presiding officer. - The Chairperson shall preside over every meeting of the Central Advisory Board and in his absence, the Vice-

Chairperson shall preside, but when both the Chairperson and the Vice-Chairperson are absent from any meeting, the members present shall elect one of the members to preside over that meeting.

24. Quorum.

(1) One-third of the total members of the Central Advisory Board shall form the quorum for any meeting.

(2) If time fixed for any meeting or during the course of any meeting, less than one-third of the total members are present, the Chairperson may adjourn the meeting to such hours on the following or on some other future date as he may fix.

(3) No quorum shall be necessary for the adjourned meeting.

(4) No matter, which had not been on the agenda of the ordinary or the special meeting, as the case may be, shall be discussed at adjourned meeting.

25. Minutes.

(1) The Member-Secretary shall maintain the record containing the names of members who attended the meeting and of the proceedings at the meetings in a book to be kept for that purpose.

(2) The minutes of the previous meeting shall be read at the beginning of the every succeeding meeting, and shall be confirmed and signed by the presiding officer at such meeting.

(3) The proceedings shall be open to inspection by any member at the office of the Member-Secretary during office hours.

26. Business to be transacted at meeting. - Except with the permission of the presiding officer, no business which is not entered in the agenda or of which notice has not been given by a member under sub-rule (5) of rule 22 shall be transacted at any meeting.

27. Agenda for the meeting of the Central Advisory Board.

(1) The business of the meeting shall be transacted in the order in which it is entered in the agenda, unless otherwise resolved in the meeting with the permission of the presiding officer.

(2) At the beginning of the meeting or after the conclusion of the debate on a motion during the meeting, the presiding officer or a member may suggest a change in the order of business as entered in

the agenda and if the Chairperson agrees, such a change shall take place.

28. **Decision by majority.** - All questions considered at a meeting of the Committee shall be decided by a majority of votes of the members present and voting and in the event of equality of votes, the Chairperson, or in the absence of the Chairperson, the Vice-Chairperson or in the absence of both the member presiding at the meeting, as the case may be, shall have a second or casting vote.

29. **No proceeding to be invalid due to vacancy or any defect.** - No proceeding of the Central Advisory Board shall be invalid by reason of existence of any vacancy in or any defect in the constitution of the Board.

CHAPTER IX

Chief Commissioner and Commissioner for Persons with Disabilities

30. **Qualification for appointment of Chief Commissioner.** - No person shall be eligible for appointment as Chief Commissioner, unless -

(a) he is a Graduate from a recognized University:
Provided that preference shall be given to persons having recognised degree or diploma in social work or law or management or human rights or rehabilitation or education of persons with disabilities;

(b) he is having experience of at least twenty-five years in a Group "A" level post in the Central Government or a State Government or a public sector undertaking or a semi Government or an autonomous body dealing with disability related matters or social sector or as a senior level functionary in registered national and international voluntary organizations in the field of disability or social development:
Provided that out of the total of twenty-five years of experience, he should have at least three years of experience in the field of rehabilitation or empowerment of persons with disabilities; and

(c) he has not attained the age of sixty years as on 1st January of the year of recruitment.

Note. - If he is in the service under the Central Government or a State Government, he shall seek retirement from such service before his appointment to the post.

31. **Qualification for appointment of Commissioner.** - No person shall be eligible for appointment as Commissioner, unless-

(a) he is a Graduate from a recognized University:

Provided that preference shall be given to persons having recognised degree or diploma in social work or law or management or human rights or rehabilitation or education of persons with disabilities.

(b) he is having at least twenty years experience in a Group "A" level post in the Central Government or a State Government or a public sector undertaking or a semi Government or an autonomous body dealing with disability related matters or social sector or as senior level functionary in registered national and international voluntary organizations in the field of disability or social development; and

(c) he has not attained the age of fifty-six years as on 1st January of the year of recruitment.

32. **Method of appointment of the Chief Commissioner and Commissioner.**

(1) The Central Government shall, six months before the post of Chief Commissioner is due to fall vacant, advertise in at least two national level dailies each in English and Hindi inviting applications for the post from eligible candidates fulfilling the qualifications specified in rules 30 and 31.

(2) A search-cum-selection committee shall be constituted to recommend a panel of three suitable candidates for the post of the Chief Commissioner or the Commissioner.

(3) The search-cum-selection committee shall be constituted in accordance with the instructions issued by the Government from time to time.

(4) The panel recommended by the committee may consist of persons from amongst those who have applied in response to the advertisement mentioned in sub-rule (1) and other eligible persons whom the Committee may consider suitable.

(5) The Central Government shall appoint one of the candidates recommended by the search-cum-selection committee as the Chief Commissioner or the Commissioner.

33. Term of the Chief Commissioner and Commissioner.

(1) The term of office of Chief Commissioner shall be for a period of three years from the date on which he assumes office, or till he attains the age of sixty-five years, whichever is earlier.

(2) The term of office of the Commissioner shall be for a period of three years and may be extended for a period of another two years or till he attains the age of sixty years, whichever is earlier.

(3) A person may serve as Chief Commissioner or Commissioner for a maximum period of two terms subject to the condition that he has not attained the age of sixty-five years, or sixty years, respectively.

34. Salary and allowances of the Chief Commissioner and Commissioner.

(1) The Chief Commissioner shall be entitled for the salary and allowances as admissible to a Secretary to the Government of India.

(2) The Commissioner shall be entitled for the salary and allowances as admissible to a Additional Secretary to the Government of India.

(3) Where a Chief Commissioner or the Commissioner being a retired Government servant or a retired employee of any institution or autonomous body funded by the Government, is in receipt of pension in respect of such previous service, the salary admissible to him under these rules shall be reduced by the amount of the pension, and if he had received in lieu of a portion of the pension, the commuted value thereof, by the amount of such commuted portion of the pension.

35. Other terms and conditions of service of the Chief Commissioner and Commissioner.

(1) The Chief Commissioner and the Commissioner shall be entitled to such leave as is admissible to a Government servant under the Central Civil Service (Leave) Rules, 1972.

(2) The Chief Commissioner and the Commissioner shall be entitled to such leave travel concession as is admissible to a Group "A"

officer under the Central Civil Services (Leave Travel Concession) Rules, 1988.

(3) The Chief Commissioner and the Commissioner shall be entitled to such medical benefits as is admissible to a Group "A" officer under the Central Government Health Scheme.

36. Resignation and removal.

(1) The Chief Commissioner and the Commissioner may, by notice in writing, under his hand, addressed to the Central Government, resign from the office:

Provided that he shall continue in the office till his resignation is accepted.

(2) The Central Government may remove a person from the office of the Chief Commissioner and the Commissioner, if he -

(a) becomes an undischarged insolvent;

(b) engages during his term of office in any paid employment or activity outside the duties of his office;

(c) is convicted or sentenced to imprisonment for an offence which in the opinion of the Central Government involves moral turpitude;

(d) is in the opinion of the Central Government, unfit to continue in office by reason of infirmity of mind or body or serious default in the performance of his functions as laid down in the Act;

(e) without obtaining leave of absence from the Central Government, remains absent from duty for a consecutive period of fifteen days or more; or

(f) has, in the opinion of the Central Government, so abused the position of the Chief Commissioner and Commissioner as to render his continuance in office detrimental to the interest of persons with disability:

Provided that no person shall be removed under this rule except after following the procedure, *mutatis mutandis*, applicable for removal of a Group "A" employee of the Central Government.

(3) The Central Government may suspend the Chief Commissioner and the Commissioner, in respect of whom proceedings for removal have been commenced in accordance with sub-rule (2), pending conclusion of such proceedings.

37. **Residuary provision.** - The conditions of service of the Chief Commissioner and the Commissioner in respect of which no express provision has been made in these rules shall be determined by the rules and orders for the time being applicable to the Secretary and Additional Secretary to the Government of India, as the case may be.

38. **Procedure to be followed by Chief Commissioner and Commissioner.**

(1) An aggrieved person may present a complaint containing the following particulars in person or by his agent to the Chief Commissioner or the Commissioner or send it by registered post or by email addressed to the Chief Commissioner or the Commissioner, namely:-
   (a) the name, description and the address of the aggrieved person;
   (b) the name, description and the address of the opposite party or parties, as the case may be, so far as they may be ascertained;
   (c) the facts relating to complaint and when and where it arose;
   (d) documents in support of the allegations contained in the complaint; and
   (e) the relief which the aggrieved person claims.

(2) The Chief Commissioner or the Commissioner on receipt of a complaint shall refer a copy of the complaint to the opposite party or parties mentioned in the complaint, directing him to give his version of the case within a period of thirty days or such extended period not exceeding fifteen days as may be granted by the Chief Commissioner or the Commissioner.

(3) On the date of hearing or any other date to which hearing could be adjourned, the parties or their agents shall appear before the Chief Commissioner or the Commissioner.

(4) Where the aggrieved person or his agent fails to appear before the Chief Commissioner or the Commissioner on such days, the Chief Commissioner or the Commissioner may either dismiss the complaint on default or decide on merits.

(5) Where the opposite party or his agent fails to appear on the date of hearing, the Chief Commissioner or the Commissioner may take such necessary action under section 77 of the Act as he deems fit for summoning and enforcing the attendance of the opposite party.

(6) The Chief Commissioner or the Commissioner may dispose of the complaint *ex-parte*, if necessary.

(7) The Chief Commissioner or the Commissioner may on such terms as he deems fit and at any stage of the proceedings, adjourn the hearing of the complaint.

(8) The Chief Commissioner or the Commissioner shall decide the complaint as far as possible within a period of three months from the date of receipt of notice by the opposite party.

39. Advisory Committee to assist the Chief Commissioner.

(1) The Central Government shall appoint an Advisory Committee comprising of the following members, namely:-

(a) five experts to represent each of the five groups of specified disabilities mentioned in the Schedule to the Act of whom two shall be women;

(b) three experts in the field of barrier-free environment-

(i) one expert from physical environment;

(ii) one expert from transportation system; and

(iii) one expert from information and communication technology or other services and facilities provided to the public;

(c) one expert in the area of employment of persons with disabilities;

(d) one legal expert; and

(e) one expert as recommended by the Chief Commissioner for Persons with Disabilities.

(2) The Chief Commissioner may invite subject or domain expert as per the need who shall assist him in meeting or hearing and in preparation of the report.

(3) The tenure of the members of the Advisory Committee shall be for a period of three years and the members shall not be eligible for re-nomination.

(4) The non-official members of the Advisory Committee, in Delhi, shall be paid an allowance of rupees two thousand per day for each day of the actual meeting.

(5) The non-official members of the Advisory Committee, not residing in Delhi, shall be paid daily allowance and travelling allowance for each day of the actual meeting at the rate admissible to a Group "A" officer of the Central Government.

40. Submission of Annual Report.

(1) The Chief Commissioner, shall as soon as possible, after the end of the financial year but not later than the 30th day of September in the next year ensuing prepare and submit to the Central Government, an annual report giving a complete account of his activities during the said financial year.

(2) In particular, the annual report referred to in sub-rule (1) shall contain information in respect of each of the following matters, namely:-

(a) names of its officers and staff and a chart showing the organisational set up;

(b) the functions which the Chief Commissioner has been empowered under sections 75 and 76 of the Act and the highlights of the performance in this regard;

(c) the main recommendations made by the Chief Commissioner;

(d) the progress made in the implementation of the Act; and

(e) any other matter deemed appropriate for inclusion by the Chief Commissioner or specified by the Central Government from time to time.

CHAPTER X

National Fund for Persons with Disabilities

41. Management of National Fund.

(1) There shall be a governing body consisting of following members to manage the National Fund, namely:-

(a) Secretary, Department of Empowerment of Persons with Disabilities, in the Central Government - Chairperson;

(b) Chairperson, Board of National Trust for the Welfare of Persons with Autism, Cerebral Palsy, Mental Retardation and Multiple Disabilities - Member;

(c) Financial Advisor, Ministry of Social Justice and Empowerment, in the Central Government - Member;

(d) two representatives from the Ministry of Health and Family Welfare, Department of School Education and Literacy, Department of Higher Education, Ministry of Labour and Employment, Department of Financial Services and Department of Rural Development in the Central Government, not below the rank of a Joint Secretary, by rotation in alphabetical order - Members;

(e) two persons representing different types of disabilities to be nominated by the Central Government, by rotation - Members;

(f) Joint Secretary in the Department of Empowerment of Persons with Disabilities in the Central Government - Convener and Chief Executive Officer.

(2) The governing body shall meet as often as necessary, but at least once in every financial year.

(3) The nominated members shall hold office for not more than three years.

(4) No member of the governing body shall be a beneficiary of the Fund during the period such member holds office.

(5) The nominated non-official members shall be eligible for payment of travelling allowance and daily allowance as admissible to a

Group `A' employees of the Central Government for attending the meetings of the governing body.

(6)   No person shall be nominated under clause (e) of sub-rule (1) as a member of the governing body if he -

(a)   is, or has been, convicted of an offence, which in the opinion of the Central Government, involves moral turpitude; or

(b)   is, or at any time has been, adjudicated as an insolvent.

42.   Utilisation of the National Fund.

(1)   The amount available under the Trust Fund for empowerment of persons with disabilities and the National Fund for people with disabilities, as on the date of the commencement of the Act, shall form the National Fund.

(2)   All monies available under the two Funds referred to in sub-rule (1) shall stand transferred to the National Fund.

(3)   All monies belonging to the Fund shall be deposited in such banks or invested in such manner as the governing body, may, subject to the general guidelines of the Central Government, decide.

(4)   The Fund shall be invested in such manner as may be decided by the governing body.

(5)   The Fund shall be utilized for the following purposes, namely:-

(a)   financial assistance in the areas which are not specifically covered under any scheme and programme of the Central Government or are not adequately funded under any scheme or programme of the Central Government;

(b)   for the purpose of implementation of the provisions of the Act;

(c)   administrative and other expenses of the Fund, as may be required to be incurred by or under this Act; and

(d)   such other purposes as may be decided by the governing body.

(6)   Every proposal of expenditure shall be placed before the governing body for its approval.

(7) The governing body may appoint secretarial staff including accountants, with such terms and conditions, as it may think appropriate, to look after the management and utilisation of the Fund.

43. **Budget.** - The Chief Executive Officer of the Fund shall prepare the budget for incurring expenditure under the Fund for each financial year showing the estimated receipt and expenditure of the Fund, in January every year and shall place the same for consideration of the governing body.

44. **Annual Report.** - The annual report of the Department of Empowerment of Persons with Disabilities shall include a chapter on National Fund.

Form I
(Persons with Disabilities Employer's Return)
[See rule 13 (1)]

Six monthly return to be submitted to the Special Employment Exchange for the half year ended _______________________________

Name and Address of the Employer _______________________________

Whether - _______________________________

Head Office _______________________________

____

Branch Office _______________________________

Nature of business/ principal activity: _______________________________

1. **Employment**

    (a) Total number of persons including working proprietors/ partners/ commission agents/ contingent paid and contractual workers, on the pay rolls of the Government establishment excluding part-time workers and apprentices. (The figures should include every person whose wage or salary is paid by the Government establishment).

On the last working day of the previous half year				
Blindness and low vision	Deaf and hard of hearing	Locomotive disability including cerebral palsy, leprosy cured, dwarfism, acid attack victims and muscular dystrophy	Autism, intellectual disability, specific learning disability and mental illness	Multiple disabilities from amongst persons with disabilities under columns (1) to (4) including deaf-blindness
(1)	(2)	(3)	(4)	(5)

On the last working day of the half year under report				
Blindness and low vision	Deaf and hard of hearing	Locomotive disability including cerebral palsy, leprosy cured, dwarfism, acid attack victims and muscular dystrophy	Autism, intellectual disability, specific learning disability and mental illness	Multiple disabilities from amongst persons with disabilities under columns (1) to (4) including deaf-blindness
(1)	(2)	(3)	(4)	(5)

Men with disability

Women with disability

Total ____

(b) Please indicate the main reasons for any increase or decrease in employment if the increase or decrease is more than 5% during the half year.

2. Vacancies. - Vacancies carrying total emoluments as per prevailing minimum wage per month and of over six months duration.

(a) Number of vacancies occurred and notified during the half year and the number filled during the half year (Separate figures may be given for men with disability and women with disability).

Number of vacancies which come within the purview of the Act.

Occurred   Notified   Filled   Source

(Describe the source from which filled)

Local/ Special Employment Exchange   General Employment Exchange

(b) Reasons for not notifying all vacancies occurred during the half year under report *vide* 2(a) ....

3.   Manpower Shortages

Vacancies/ posts unfilled because of shortage of suitable applicants.

Name of the occupation or Designation of the posts	Number of unfilled vacancies/ posts		disability wise experience not necessary
	essential qualification	essential experience	
1	2	3	4

Please list any other occupations for which this Government establishment had recently any difficulty in obtaining suitable applicants.

Dated ………………….   Signature of employer

To

The Employment Exchange

———————————————-

———————————————

Note. - This return relates to half yearly ending 31st March/ 30th September and shall be rendered to the local Special Employment Exchange within thirty days after the end of the half year concerned.

Form II
(Persons with Disabilities Employer's Return)
[See rule 13 (1)]
Occupational return to be submitted to the local Special Employment Exchange once in two years.

Name and Address of the Employer ______________________________

Nature of business _______________________________________

(describe what the Government establishment makes or does as its principal activity)

1. Total number of persons on the pay rolls of the Government establishment on (Specify date) .... (This figure should include every person whose wage or salary is paid by the Government establishment)(Separate figures for men with disability and women with disability may be given).

2. Occupational classification of all employees as given in item - 1 above.

(please give below the number of employees in each occupation separately)

Occupation	Number of Employees			
Use exact terms	Men with disability	Women with disability	Total	
Such as Engineer (Mechanical); Teacher (domestic/ science); Officer on duty (actuary); Assistant Director (Metallurgist); Scientific Assistant (chemist); Research Officer (economist); Instructor (carpenter);				Please give as far as possible approximate number of vacancies in each occupation you are likely to fill during the next calendar year due to retirement.

Occupation	Number of Employees			
Supervisor(tailor);				
Fitter(internal)				
Combustion (engine);				
Inspector Sanitary);				
Superintendent Office;				
apprentice (Electrician).				
Total				
Dated …………………………..				Signature of employer

To

The Employment Exchange

(please fill in here the address of your local Special Employment Exchange)

Note: Total of column 5 under item 2 should correspond to the figure given against item-1.

Form III
(Persons with Disabilities Employer's Return)
[*See* rule 14]

Name and Address of the Employer _______________________

Whether - Head Office _______________________

Branch Office _______________________

Nature of business/ principal activity: _______________________

Total number of persons on the pay rolls of the Government establishment (This figure should include every person whose wage or salary is paid by the Government establishment).

Total number of persons with disabilities (disability-wise) on the payroll of the Government establishment. (This figure should include every person with disability whose wage or salary is paid by the Government establishment).

(a) Occupational qualification of all employees (Please give below the number of employees in each occupation separately.

Occupation	Number of Employees			
Use exact terms	Men with disability	Women with disability	Total	
Such as Engineer (Mechanical); Teacher (domestic/ science); Officer on duty (actuary); Assistant Director (Metallurgist); Scientific Assistant (chemist); Research Officer (economist); Instructor (carpenter);				Please give as far as possible approximate number of vacancies in each occupation you are likely to fill during the next calendar year due to retirement.
Total				

(b) Please indicate the main reasons for any increase or decrease in employment if the increase or decrease is more than 5% during the half year

2. Vacancies: Vacancies carrying total emoluments as per prevailing minimum wage per month and of over six months duration.

(a) Number of vacancies occurred and notified during the half year and the number filled during the half year.

Number of vacancies which come within the purview of the Act				
Occurred	Notified Local Special Employment Exchange	General employment	Filled	Sources (Describe the source form which filled
1	2	3	4	5
Total				

(b) Reasons for not notifying all vacancies occurred during the half year under report *vide* (a) 2 .... above.

3. Manpower shortages

Vacancies/ posts unfilled because of shortage of suitable applications			
Name of the occupation or Designation of the posts	Number of unfiled vacancies/ posts		Experience Not necessary
	Essential qualification	Essential experience	
1.	2.	3.	4.

Please list any other occupations for which this Government establishment had recently any difficulty in obtaining suitable applicants.

Dated ....   Signature of employer

Form IV
Application for Obtaining Certificate of Disability by Persons with Disabilities
[See rule 17(1)]

(1) Name: __________ __________ __________

          (Surname)   (First Name)   (Middle Name)

(2) Father's Name: ________________ Mother's Name: ________________

(3) Date of Birth: __________/ __________/ __________

          (Date)   (Month)   (Year)

(4) Age at the time of application: ________________ years

(5) Sex: Male/ Female/ Transgender ________________

(6) Address:

    (a) Permanent address   (b) Current Address (i.e. for communication)

    ________________   ________________

    ________________   ________________

    (c) Period since when residing at current address   ________________

(7) Educational Status (please tick as applicable)

    (i) Post Graduate

    (ii) Graduate

    (iii) Diploma

    (iv) Higher Secondary

    (v) High School

    (vi) Primary

    (viii) Non-literate

(8) Occupation ______________________

(9) Identification marks (i) ________________ (ii) ________________

(10) Nature of disability:

(11) Period since when disabled: From Birth/ / since year __________

(12) (i) Did you ever apply for issue of a certificate of disability in the past ___ yes/ no

    (ii) If yes, details:

       (a) Authority to whom and district in which applied

       ________________ ______________

       (b) Result of application ______________________________

(13) Have you ever been issued a certificate of disability in the past? If yes, please enclose a true copy.

Declaration: I hereby declare that all particulars stated above are true to the best of my knowledge and belief, and no material information has been concealed or misstated. I further state that if any inaccuracy is detected in the application, I shall be liable to forfeiture of any benefits derived and other action as per law.

____

(signature or left thumb impression of person with disability, or of his/ her legal guardian in case of persons with intellectual disability, autism, cerebral palsy and multiple disabilities, etc)

Date:

Place:

Enclosures:

1. Proof of residence (Please tick as applicable).

    (a) ration card,

    (b) voter identity card,

    (c) driving license,

    (d) bank passbook,

    (e) PAN card,

    (f) passport,

    (g) telephone, electricity, water and any other utility bill indicating the address of the applicant,

(h) a certificate of residence issued by a Panchayat, municipality, cantonment board, any gazetted officer, or the concerned Patwari or Head Master of a Government school,

(i) in case of an inmate of a residential institution for persons with disabilities, destitute, mentally ill, and other disability, a certificate of residence from head of such institution.

2. Two recent passport size photographs

____

____

(For office use only)

Date:

Place:

Signature of issuing authority Stamp

Form V
Certificate of Disability
(In cases of amputation or complete permanent paralysis of limbs
or dwarfism and in case of blindness)
[See rule 18(1)]

(Name and Address of the Medical Authority issuing the Certificate)

Recent passport
size attested
photograph
(Showing face
only) of the person
with disability.

Certificate No.   Date:

This   is   to   certify   that   I   have   carefully   examined
Shri/ Smt. / Kum. ____
son/ wife/ daughter of Shri _________________________________
Date of Birth (DD/ MM/ YY) ____________ Age ______ years,
male/ female ____________ registration No. ______________
permanent resident of House No. ___________ Ward/ Village/
Street ____________ Post Office _________ District _________
State __________ , whose photograph is affixed above, and am satisfied
that:

(A) he/ she is a case of:

    ➤   locomotor disability

    ➤   dwarfism

    ➤   blindness

   (Please tick as applicable)

(B) the diagnosis in his/ her case is ____________

(C) he/ she has____________% (in figure)_______________ percent (in words) permanent locomotor disability/ dwarfism/ blindness in relation to his/ her ________ (part of body) as per guidelines (................. number and date of issue of the guidelines to be specified).

2. The applicant has submitted the following document as proof of residence:-

Nature of Document	Date of Issue	Details of authority issuing certificate

(Signature and Seal of Authorised Signatory
of notified Medical Authority)

Signature/ thumb impression of the person in whose favour certificate of disability is issued.

Form VI

Certificate of Disability
(In cases of multiple disabilities)
[See rule 18(1)]

(Name and Address of the Medical Authority issuing the Certificate)

<table>
<tr><td>Recent passport size attested photograph (Showing face only) of the person with disability.</td></tr>
</table>

Certificate No.	Date:

This is to certify that we have carefully examined Shri/ Smt. / Kum. ____

son/ wife/ daughter of Shri ______________________________________

Date of Birth (DD/ MM/ YY) _____________ Age _____ years, male/ female _______________. Registration No. _________ permanent resident of House No. ____________ Ward/Village/ Street ____________ Post Office ____________ District ____________ State _____________, whose photograph is affixed above, and am satisfied that:

(A) he/ she is a case of Multiple Disability. His/ her extent of permanent physical impairment/ disability has been evaluated as per guidelines (........................ number and date of issue of the guidelines to be specified) for the disabilities ticked below, and is shown against the relevant disability in the table below:

Sl. No.	Disability	Affected part of body	Diagnosis	Permanent physical impairment/ mental disability (in%)
1.	Locomotor disability	@		
2.	Muscular Dystrophy			
3.	Leprosy cured			
4.	Dwarfism			
5.	Cerebral Palsy			
6.	Acid attack Victim			
7.	Low vision	#		
8.	Blindness	#		
9.	Deaf	£		
10.	Hard of Hearing	£		
11.	Speech and Language disability			
12.	Intellectual Disability			
13.	Specific Learning Disability			
14.	Autism Spectrum Disorder			
15.	Mental illness			
16.	Chronic Neurological Conditions			
17.	Multiple sclerosis			
18.	Parkinson's disease			
19.	Haemophilia			
20.	Thalassemia			
21.	Sickle Cell disease			

(B) In the light of the above, his/ her over all permanent physical impairment as per guidelines (.................. number and date of issue of the guidelines to be specified), is as follows: -

In figures: - ——————————— percent

In words: - ———- percent

2. This condition is progressive/ non-progressive/ likely to improve/ not likely to improve.

3. Reassessment of disability is:

   (i)   not necessary, or

   (ii) is recommended/ after .... years .... months, and therefore this certificate shall be valid till ——- ——- ——— (DD) (MM) (YY)

   @ e.g. Left/ right/ both arms/ legs

   # e.g. Single eye

   £ e.g. Left/ Right/ both ears

4. The applicant has submitted the following document as proof of residence:-

Nature of document	Date of issue	Details of authority issuing certificate

5. Signature and seal of the Medical Authority.

Name and Seal of Member	Name and Seal of Member	Name and Seal of the Chairperson

Signature/ thumb impression of the person in whose favour certificate of disability is issued.

Form VII
Certificate of Disability
(In cases other than those mentioned in Forms V and VI)
(Name and Address of the Medical Authority issuing the Certificate)
[See rule 18(1)]

> Recent passport size attested photograph (Showing face only) of the person with disability.

Certificate No.   Date:

This is to certify that I have carefully examined

Shri/ Smt/ Kum ____

son/ wife/ daughter of Shri _______________________________________

Date of Birth (DD/ MM/ YY)___________Age ________ years, male/

female __________ Registration No. _____________ permanent

resident of House No. _____________ Ward/ Village/ Street

_________________ Post Office ___________ District ___________

State _______________, whose photograph is affixed above, and am

satisfied that he/ she is a case of _________________ disability. His/

her extent of percentage physical impairment/ disability has been

evaluated as per guidelines (................. number and date of issue

of the guidelines to be specified) and is shown against the relevant

disability in the table below:-

Sl. No.	Disability	Affected part of body	Diagnosis	Permanent physical impairment/ mental disability (in%)
1.	Locomotor disability	@		
2.	Muscular Dystrophy			
3.	Leprosy cured			
4.	Cerebral Palsy			
5.	Acid attack Victim			
6.	Low vision	#		
7.	Deaf	€		
8.	Hard of Hearing	€		
9.	Speech and Language disability			
10.	Intellectual Disability			
11.	Specific Learning Disability			
12.	Autism Spectrum Disorder			
13.	Mental illness			
14.	Chronic Neurological Conditions			
15.	Multiple sclerosis			
16.	Parkinson's disease			
17.	Haemophilia			
18.	Thalassemia			
19.	Sickle Cell disease			

(Please strike out the disabilities which are not applicable)

2. The above condition is progressive/ non-progressive/ likely to improve/ not likely to improve.

3.   Reassessment of disability is:

   (i)   not necessary, or

   (ii) is recommended/ after _________ years _________________ months, and therefore this certificate shall be valid till (DD/ MM/ YY) ____ ____ ____

   @ - eg. Left/ Right/ both arms/ legs

   # - eg. Single eye/ both eyes

   € - eg. Left/ Right/ both ears

4.   The applicant has submitted the following document as proof of residence:-

Nature of Document	Date of Issue	Details of authority issuing certificate

(Authorised Signatory of notified Medical Authority)

(Name and Seal)

Countersigned

{Countersignature and seal of the

Chief Medical Officer/ Medical Superintendent/

Head of Government Hospital, in case the

Certificate is issued by a medical authority who is

not a Government servant (with seal)}

<table><tr><td>Signature/ thumb impression of the person in whose favour certificate of disability is issued.</td></tr></table>

Note. - In case this certificate is issued by a medical authority who is not a Government servant, it shall be valid only if countersigned by the Chief Medical Officer of the District

Form VIII
[Intimation of rejection of Application for Certificate of Disability]
[See rule 18 (4)]

No. ___________________   Dated:

To,

(Name and address of applicant for Certificate of Disability)

Sub: Rejection of Application for Certificate of Disability

Sir/ Madam,

Please refer to your application dated ___________ for issue of a Certificate of Disability for the following disability: _____________

2. Pursuant to the above application, you have been examined by the undersigned/ Medical Authority on _________, and I regret to inform that, for the reasons mentioned below, it is not possible to issue a Certificate of Disability in your favour:

   (i)

   (ii)

   (iii)

3. In case you are aggrieved by the rejection of your application, you may represent to___________, requesting for review of this decision.

Yours faithfully,

(Authorised Signatory of the notified Medical Authority)

(Name and Seal)

Ministry of Statistics & Programme Implementation

NSS report no. 583: Persons with Disabilities in India NSS 76th round (July – December 2018)

Posted On: 23 NOV 2019 5:17PM by PIB Delhi

The National Statistical Office (NSO), Ministry of Statistics and Programme Implementation has conducted a Survey of Persons with Disabilities during July 2018 to December 2018 as a part of 76th round of National Sample Survey (NSS). Prior to this, survey on the same subject was carried out by NSO during the 58th round (July-December 2002).

2. The main objective of the *Survey of Persons with Disabilities* conducted by NSO in its 76th round was to estimate indicators of incidence and prevalence of disability, cause of disability, age at onset of disability, facilities available to the persons with disability, difficulties faced by persons with disability in accessing/using public building/public transport, arrangement of regular care giver, out-of pocket expenses relating to disability, etc. In NSS 76th round survey, for classification of disabilities, all the specified disabilities as stated in *The Rights of Persons with Disabilities Act, 2016* have been considered.

3. The present survey was spread across the country and for the central sample, data were collected from 1,18,152 households (81,004 in rural areas and 37,148 in urban areas) and 5,76,569 persons (4,02,589 in rural areas and 1,73,980 in urban areas), following a scientific survey methodology, were enumerated. In this survey, total number of persons with disability surveyed was 1,06,894 (74,946 in rural areas and 31,948 in urban areas) persons

with disabilities were surveyed. The report is based on the central sample data of the *Survey of Persons with Disabilities* during NSS 76th round. Some important findings of the survey, based on the response of the households, are presented in the following paragraphs:

3.1 Prevalence and incidence of disability

a. In India prevalence of disability (percentage of persons with disability in the population) was 2.2% with 2.3% in rural and 2.0% in urban areas.

b. Prevalence of disability was higher among males than females. Among males, prevalence of disability was 2.4% while it was 1.9% among females.

c. Incidence of disability in the population, that is the number of persons with onset of disability (by birth or otherwise) during 365 days preceding the date of survey was 86 per 1,00,000 persons.

3.2 Level of education among persons with disabilities

a. Among persons with disabilities of age 7 years and above, 52.2% were literate.

b. Among persons with disabilities of age 15 years and above, 19.3% had highest educational level as secondary and above.

c. Among persons with disabilities of age 3 to 35 years, 10.1% attended pre-school intervention programme.

d. Percentage of persons with disabilities of age 3 to 35 years, who were ever enrolled in ordinary school, was 62.9%.

3.3 Living arrangement, care giver, receipt of aid/help, certificate of disability

a. Percentage of persons with disabilities who were living alone[1] was 3.7%.

b. Among persons with disabilities, 62.1% had care giver, for 0.3% of the persons with disabilities caregiver was required but not available and for another 37.7% of the persons with disabilities no caregiver was required.

c.   Percentage of persons with disabilities who received aid/help from Government was 21.8% and another 1.8% received aid/help from organisations other than Government.

d.   Among persons with disabilities, 28.8% reported that they had a certificate of disability.

3.4 Labour Force Participation Rate, Worker Population Ratio and Unemployment Rate in usual status (ps+ss) among persons with disabilities

a.   Among persons with disabilities of age 15 years and above, Labour Force Participation Rate in usual status (ps+ss) was 23.8%.

b.   Among persons with disabilities of age 15 years and above, Worker Population Ratio in usual status (ps+ss) was 22.8%.

c.   Among persons with disabilities of age 15 years and above, Unemployment Rate in usual status (ps+ss) was 4.2%.

4.   The Report on the "**Survey of Persons with Disabilities**" and unit level data are both available on www.mospi.gov.in.

[1] Persons living alone were those who were living alone 'not as an inmate of institution/ hostel' or living alone 'as an inmate of institution/ hostel'

AS INTRODUCED IN LOK SABHA
Bill No. 40 of 2022
THE RIGHTS OF PERSONS WITH DISABILITIES
(AMENDMENT) BILL, 2022
By
SHRIMATI CHINTA ANURADHA, M.P.
A
BILL

further to amend the Rights of Persons with Disabilities Act, 2016.

Short title and commencement.	BE it enacted by Parliament in the Seventy-third Year of the Republic of India as follows:—

1. (1) This Act may be called the Rights of Persons with Disabilities (Amendment) Act, 2022.

   (*2*) It shall come into force on such date as the Central Government may, by notification in the Official Gazette, appoint.

Terms of office and conditions of service of Chairperson and Members.
Officers and other employees of the National Commission.
Salary, allowances and administrative expenses to be paid by the Central Government.

2. After Chapter X of the Rights of the Persons with Disabilities Act, 2016 the following Chapter and sections thereunder shall be inserted, namely:—

Insertion of new Chapter XA. Constitution of the National Commission for Persons with Disabilities.	**"59A. (*1*) The Central Government shall, as soon as may be by notification in the Gazette, constitute a body to be known as the National Commission for Persons with Disabilities, hereinafter referred to in this Chapter as the National Commission, to exercise the power and to perform the functions conferred on it under this Act.**

(2) **The Commission shall consist of the following members, namely:—**

    (a) **a Chairperson who shall be a person with disability, having special knowledge in matters relating to the disability issues and knowledge in law;**

    (b) **a member who may be a person with disability or not, having special knowledge in matters relating to the disability issues and knowledge in law;**

    (c) **a woman who may be a person with disability or not, having special knowledge in matters relating to the disability issues and knowledge in law and has proved working excellence in such matters, to be appointed by the Central Government in such manner as may be prescribed.**

(3) An officer not below the rank of an Additional Secretary to the Government of India shall be the Member–Secretary and the Chief Executive Officer of the National Commission and shall exercise such powers and discharge the functions as the National Commission may, by its order, authorize.

Terms of office and conditions of service of Chairperson and Members.

59B. (*1*) Each member may continue in office till the completion of three years from the date on which he assumes office.

(2) The Chairperson or a member of the National Commission may, at any time, by giving intimation to the Central Government in writing under his hand, demit his office.

(3) The Central Government shall remove a person from the office of the Chairperson or of a Member, if that person—

    (a) becomes an undischarged insolvent; or

    (b) has been convicted and sentenced to imprisonment for an offence which, in the opinion of the Central Government, involves moral turpitude; or

(c) becomes of unsound mind and stands so declared by a competent court; or

(d) refuses to work or becomes incapable to work; or

(e) without obtaining prior permission from the National Commission, does not attend three consecutive meetings of the National Commission; or

(f) in the opinion of the Central Government, has so abused the official position of Chairperson or Member as to render that person's continuance in office detrimental to the interest of disabled people or public interest:

Provided that no person shall be removed under this sub-section unless that person is given a reasonable opportunity of being heard in the matter.

<table>
<tr><td>Officers and other employees of the National Commission.</td><td>59C. (1) The Central Government shall provide such officers and other employees as may be required for the efficient performance of the National Commission.</td></tr>
</table>

(2) **The salary and allowances payable to, and the terms and conditions of service of the officers and other employees appointed for the purpose of the National Commission shall be such as may be prescribed.**

<table>
<tr><td>Salary, allowances and administrative expenses to be paid by the Central Government.</td><td>59D. The salary and allowances payable to the Chairperson and Members, and the administrative expenses, including salary, allowances and pension payable to the officers and other employees referred to in sub-section (1) of section 59(C), shall be paid by the Central Government.</td></tr>
</table>

59E. The National Commission shall,—

Functions of the National Commission.

(a) evaluate the progress of the development of persons with disabilities in the country;

(b) enquire and monitor the manner of functioning of various safeguards provided, in the Constitution or under any other law or under any order of the Central Government for the welfare, protection and empowerment of the persons with disability in the country;

(c) enquire into specific complaints about deprivation of social, economic, educational and linguistic rights, safeguards and benefits of the persons with disabilities to bring such matters into the notice of authorities concerned and to suggest remedial measures;

(d) participate in and give creative suggestions on the planning programmes for the educational, social and economic development of the persons with disabilities;

(e) make recommendations as to the steps to be taken by the Central Government for the effective implementation of the measures and safeguards for the educational, social and economic development, welfare and protection of the persons with disabilities and to make report to the Central Government either annually or at such other time, as the National Commission may deem fit and to monitor their timely implementation;

(f) cause studies to be undertaken into various problems arising out of discrimination towards persons with disabilities and recommend measures for their removal; and

(g) conduct studies, research and analysis and to organise seminars, symposium and awareness classes on the issues relating to social, economic and educational advancement of persons with disabilities.

<table><tr><td>Supervision of issuing Certificate of Disability.</td><td>59F. In case of any difficulty relating to issue of Certificate of Disability under section 58 in the manner and form specified by the Central Government to the persons with disability comes to the notice of the National Commission, the National</td></tr></table>

Commission may report the same to the Central Government and suggest remedial measures therefore.

<table><tr><td>Laying of Report.</td><td>59G. The Central Government shall cause the reports referred to in section 59F, to be laid</td></tr></table>

before each House of the Parliament along with the action taken or proposed to be taken thereon and also the reasons, if any, for non-acceptance of the recommendations in such manner as may be prescribed.

<table><tr><td>Power to remove difficulties.</td><td>59H. (1) If any difficulty arises in giving effect to the provisions of this Chapter, the Central Government may, by order published in the Gazette, make</td></tr></table>

provisions not inconsistent with the provisions of this Act which appear to it to be necessary or expedient, for removing the difficulty:

Provided that no such order shall be made after the expiry of a period of two years from the date of commencement of this Act.

Every order made under this section shall, as soon as may be after it is made, be laid before the Parliament of India.".

STATEMENT OF OBJECTS AND REASONS

The Rights of Persons with Disabilities Act, 2016 was enacted to protect the rights and ensure welfare of the persons with disabilities. Under the aforesaid Act a Central Advisory Board on Disability has been constituted. However, the comprehensive social and educational advancement, welfare, protection and empowerment of persons with disability is yet to achieved.

The need is to constitute a National Commission for the Persons with Disability on the lines for the development of National Commission for the Minorities, Women, Other Backward Classes, the Scheduled Castes and the Scheduled Tribes. The establishment of the National Commission is intended to provide equality and welfare as well as the safeguard to the four per cent. of the persons with disability in the national population.

The Bill, therefore, seeks to amend the Persons with Disability Act, 2016 with a view to constitute a National Commission for Persons with Disabilities.

Hence this Bill.

NEW DELHI; CHINTA ANURADHA
16 December, 2021.

FINANCIAL MEMORANDUM

Clause 2 of the Bill *vide* proposed section 59A provides for the constitution of National Commission of Persons with Disabilities. It also provides for appointment of a Chairperson and other members of the National Commission. It also *vide* proposed section 59C provides for appointment of officers and employees to the National Commission. It further *vide* proposed section 59D provides for the salary and allowances payable to the Chairperson and members of the National Commission to be paid out of the grants available to the Central Government. The Bill if enacted will involve expenditure from the Consolidated Fund of India. A recurring expenditure of rupees one hundred crore would be involved.

A non-recurring expenditure of rupees three hundred crore would also be involved.

LOK SABHA

A

BILL

further to amend the Right of Persons with Disabilities Act, 2016.

——————

(Shrimati Chinta Anuradha, M.P.)

Disablity-a Major Human Rights Concern

QUESTIONNAIRE

1   Personal Background

    Name _______________ Age_______________ Contact No.

2   Family Background Joint Single

3. What Is Your Educational Background

4   Type Of Disability

5. Age When Disability Suffered

Professional Background

1. What Is Your Professional Or Vocational Training

2. Any Source Of Income

3. Do You Have Any Kind Of Financial Support And Assistance

4. Family

5. Society

6. Govt

7. N G O

Socio Economic Background

1. Do You Know About Your Rights and Privileges

2. Do You Think That You Are Ignored or Cared

3. What Can You Contribute for Society

4. What You Expect From Society and Govt

5. What Sort of Challenges or Problems You Have to Face

6.   Are You Capable to Face Challenges in Your Day to Day Life?
7.   How You Cope Up the Problems Faced by You
8.   What Are Your Complaints and For Whom

AWARENESS LEVEL

1.   What and Who Is Your Strength and Weaknesses
2.   What Are the Laws Relating Your Disability Cause
3.   Do You Have Knowledge About Your Human Rights
4.   What Steps Have Been Taken by Government Towards This Cause
5.   What Improvements Should Be Done
6.   Give Your Suggestions for Safety and Security from This Cause
7.   Have You Ever Complained to Any Authorities for Ur Problems
8.   Did Any Authority Respond to Redress your Grievances
9.   Any Sort of Awareness Camp Is Organized So Far
10.   Whom Do You Blame for The Inconvenience

References

- Vijaypur, Abdulrahim kumar Suresh, (1999) Perspectives on Human Rights, Manak Publications, New Delhi
- S.R. Chauhan, N.S. Chauhan (Ed.)(2005), "Disabled Persons Rights", International Dimension of Human Rights, at 335(2006).
- Shruti Pandey, Priyanka Chirmar, Deepika D'souza, Preface, Disability and the Law, at 4, (2005).
- Parsad, R.N., (1999) Human Rights in India, An analytical Perspectives, Kanishka Publishers, New Delhi. (1999)
- Grover, Dr. Anil, (2013), A Text book of Human Rights, Astha publishers, New Delhi.
- Naseema, C.(2008), Human Rights Education, Kanishka Publishers, New Delhi.
- Sinha, P.C.Global sourcebookon Human Rights Part I, Kanishka Publishers, New Delhi.
- Sinha, P.C., Global source book on Human rights part II, Kanishka publishers, New Delhi.
- Syed Mehartaj Begum, Human rights in India: Issues and Perspectives, A.P.H.Publishers, New Delhi.
- Sahu, Asima, Human rights Violations and the Law, Pointer Publishers, Jaipur.
- Dikshit, R.C., (1998), Human Rights and the Law, Universal and Indian, New Delhi: Deep ndDeep.
- Kashyap, Subhash C., (1978), Human Rights and Parliament, Delhi: Metropolitan.
- Kirpal, B.N. et al., (2004), Supreme but Not Infallible, New Delhi.
- Jha, R.C., (1995), Resurrecting: Human Right in India, Sheridan Book Company, New Delhi

- Bava, Noorjahan, (ed), (2000), Human rights and Criminal Justice Administration in India, New Delhi: Uppal Publishing House.
- Nirmal, C.J., (1999), Human Rights in India, Oxford, New Delhi
- Purkayastha, Bandana;(2012), Human Rights Voices of World's Young Activists, FrontPage Publications, London.
- Mohanty, jagannath;(2013); Human Rights Education, Deep and Deep Publications, New Delhi.
- Sehgal, B.P.Singh;(2008); Human Rights In India, DeepAnd Deep Publications, New Delhi.
- N.R.Sharma, (1999); Human Rights in the world, Pointer Publishers, Jaipur
- Khare Subhash Chander, (1977), Human Rights and, Metropolitan Book, New Delhi.
- Iyer, Justice VR Krishna, (1984), Human Right and the Law, VedPa lLaw House, Indore.
- Begum, Dr. S. Mehartaj, (2010), Human Rights in India, A.P.H.Publishing Corporation, New Delhi.
- Internet sources: Human rights watch
- http://www1.umn.edu/humanrts/edumat/hreduseries/hrhandbook/part1D.html
- http://www.why.do/why-do-we-need-human-rights/
- www.humanrights.is/english/qa/
- Internet Sources
- Basu Durga Das, (1997) Introduction to the Constitution of India, Prentice Hall of India, New Delhi, 1997
- Mehta, P. L. and Neena Verma, (1995), Human Rights Under the Indian Constitutions, New Delhi: Deep and Deep Publications.
- Kumar, Bindal, (2000), Problems of Working Children, APH Publication, New Delhi
- Ghosh, S.K., (1993), Torture and Rape in Police Custody, : Asish Publishing House, New Delhi
- Sharma, A.K. (1995) "Human Rights Violations of Street Children and Child Labor in New Delhi", In B. P. Singh Seghal (ed.) Human Rights in India: Problems and Perspectives, Deep and Deep, NewDelhi.

- Singh, S.K., (1994), Bonded Labor and the La, Deep and Deep. New Delh

- Siddiqi and Ranganathan, hand Book on Women and Human Rights: a guide for Social Activities, Part I, kanishka Publishers, New Delhi.

- Siddiqi and Ranganathan, Hand Book on women and Human Rights: A Guide For Social Activities Part II, kaniishka Pblishers, New Delhi.

- Akhilesh Das, Swastic Publications, Delhi Human Rights Education in 21st century,

- Dr. K.V.RaviKumar, Kanishka Publishers, New Delhi Human Rights in Demographic Perspective Promotion And Protection of Human Rights,

- Jayant Chowdhary, Hand Book of Human Rights, Wisdom Press, New Delhi

- Mohd Yasin Ahmed, Hand Book of Constitutional Human rights, Hand Book of Human Rights, Astha Publishers New Delhi

- Suresh Kumar Tayagi, Human rights and Democratization, Swastic Publications, Delhi,

- Anand Kumar Sharma, Measuring Human rights Principles, Practice and policy, Swastic publications, Delhi

- D.K.Samantroy, Hand Book of Human rights and social justice, Measuring Human rights Principles, Practice and policy, Astha publications, Delhi

- S.C.kataria, Astha Role of NGOS in Protecting Human Rights, Publications Delhi

- Dinesh Singh, Human rights development in India, Rathore Black Printers, New Delhi

- D.K.Wadhwa and M.k. Singh, Encyclopedia of Human Rights, Surendra Publications, New Delhi

- D.k.Wadhwa and M.K.Singh, Encyclopedia of human rights, Surendra Publications, New Delhi

- Surendra khanna, Democracy and human rights, Swastic Publications, Delhi

- Gopal Ram Dass, International provisions of Human rights, Swastic Publications, New Delhi
- Satya P.kanan, Human Rights and gender Justice, An Overview, Human rights Dimensions, Wisdom Press, Delhi
- Dinesh Singh Rathore, Dalit and Human rights, Black Prints, Delhi
- Anil Grover, A Text book of Human Rights, Aastha Publishers, New Delhi
- Saud Akhtar, Pramod Kumar Human Rights in the World, Sarup Book Publisher, New Delhi
- Kuldeep Singh, Human Rigths and Social Justice, Sonali Publisheers, New Delhi
- Satya P.Kanan, Human Rights Evolution and Development Wisdom press, Delhi
- Saud Akhtar, Pramod Kumar, Human Rights in India, sarup Book Publishers, New Delhi
- Satya P.Kanan, Global human Rights: Issues and Initiatives, Widsdom Press, New Delhi
- Ramesh Thakur, Dialogue on Expanding horizons of Human rights, Cyber Tech publications New Delhi, Vol.I
- Ramesh Thakur, Dialogue on Expanding horizons of Human rights, Cyber Tech publications New Delhi, Vol.II
- Ramesh Thakur, Dialogue on Expanding horizons of Human rights Cyber Tech publications New Delhi, Vol.III
- A.S. Kohli, Human rights and social work Kanishka Publishers, New Delhi
- Trilok Sharma, Dalit, and Human Rights, Sonali Publications, New Delhi
- Gopal D.pandey, Human Rights Past, present and Future, Swastic Publishers Delhi, Vol I
- Gopal D.pandey, Human Rights Past, present and Future, Swastic Publishers Delhi, Vol II
- R.V.Prasad Human Rights in India, Kanishka Publishers, New Delhi
- Akhilesh Das, Human Rights Democracy and Globalised World order, Swastik Publishers, Delhi

- Journal On Developmental Disabilities, Volume 10, Number 2 1 Human Rights and Disability: The International Context
- International Journal of Law and Legal Jurisprudence Studies: ISSN:2348-8212 Volume 2 Issue 1 Published By: Universal Multidisciplinary Research Institute Pvt Ltd; Differently abled Persons and Human Rights: Issues and Responses Amritpal Kaur
- MacLachlan, Malcolm, 2016, Disability and Human Rights NOT FOR DISTRIBUTION, Palgrave Macmillan in the US is a division of St Martin's Press LLC, 175 Fifth Avenue, New York, NY 10010
- Gerard Quinn, and Theresia Degener. *Human Rights and Disability*. New York and Geneva: United Nations, 2002, p. 14. [Google Scholar]
- Michael Oliver. Understanding Disability. New York: St. Martin's Press, 1996. [Google Scholar]
- Theresia Degener. "A human rights model of disability." In *Routledge Handbook of Disability Law and Human Rights*. Edited by Blanck Peter and Flynn Eilionoir. London and New York: Routledge, 2017, pp. 31–50.
- Jerome Bickenbach. *Physical Disability and Social Policy*. Toronto, Buffalo and London: University of Toronto Press, 1992.

Disability Networks on The Web:

- Action Aid: http://www.facebook.com/ActionAidIndia
- World Health Organisation: http://www.facebook.com/WHO
- Bodies of Work: http://www.facebook.com/BodiesOfWork
- NALSAR: http://facebook.com/pages/…Disability-Studies-Nalsar.
- Samarthayam- National Centre for Accessible Environments: www.facebook.com/samarthyamuniversalaccess
- Centre for Disability Studies: http://facebook.com/UDelCDS
- ABILITY INT: http://www.abilityint.co.uk/
- DoingDisability:http://www.facebook.com/events/1429375020611446/
- Disability Rights Education and Defense Fund: http://www.facebook.com/DREDE.org

- Rajesh Speaks: http://www.facebook.com/Rajesh Speaks. HumanRights
- Access Ability: http://www.facebook.com/abilityindiana
- Institute on Disability and Human Development: http://www.uic. edu/depts/idhd/
- Representing Disability in An Albeist World: www.avocadopress.org/
- University of Illinois at Chicago: www.ahs.uic.edu/dhd/
- Disability Cultural Centre- Syracuse University: www.sudcc.syr.edu
- Paul K. Longmore Institute on Disability: www.longmoreinstitute. sfsu.edu/pages/aboutinstitute
- http://www.un.org/disabilities/documents/gadocs/a_c.3_70_l.56. pdf (accessed on 19 August 2016).
- Society for Disability Studies: www.disstudies.org
- https://papers.ssrn.com/sol3/papers.cfm?abstract_id=1732128
- https://disabilityaffairs.gov.in/content/
- https://www.drishtiias.com/to-the-points/Paper2/issues-related-to-persons-with-disability
- https://www.drishtiias.com/to-the-points/Paper2/issues-related-to-persons-with-disability
- https://www.ohrc.on.ca/en/policy-ableism-and-discrimination-based-disability/2-what-disability
- https://www.statista.com/topics/8278/disabilities-in-india/#editorsPicks
- https://www.legalserviceindia.com/legal/article-33-the-rights-of-the-disabled-.html
- https://impart.snehadhara.org/wp-content/uploads/Policies/Legislation_and_Disability_Policy_of_Central_Government.pdf
- https://www.legalservicesindia.com/article/163/Right-Of-Disabled.html#google_vignette
- https://thediplomat.com/2016/12/the-history-of-indias-disability-rights-movement/
- http://ijrar.com/upload_issue/ijrar_issue_20543326.pdf
- https://sparsh.mp.gov.in/Public/SparshPublicPages/ActsInDisability. aspx

- https://www.mospi.gov.in/sites/default/files/reports_and_publication/statistical_publication/social_statistics/Chapter%204-Dimension_Disability.pdf
- https://pib.gov.in/PressReleasePage.aspx?PRID=1593253
- https://ruralindiaonline.org/en/library/resource/persons-with-disabilities-divyangjan-in-india—-a-statistical-profile-2021/